RECORDED VERSIONS
GUITAR

AUTHENTIC TRANSCRIPTIONS
WITH NOTES AND TABLATURE

FLYLEAF

Music transcriptions by Jeff Story

ISBN-13: 978-1-4234-2129-0
ISBN-10: 1-4234-2129-9

HAL•LEONARD®
CORPORATION
7777 W. BLUEMOUND RD. P.O. BOX 13819 MILWAUKEE, WI 53213

Visit Hal Leonard Online at
www.halleonard.com

I'm So Sick

Words and Music by Sameer Bhattacharya, Jared Hartmann, Kirkpatrick Seals, James Culpepper and Lacey Mosley

Drop D tuning:
(low to high) D-A-D-G-B-E

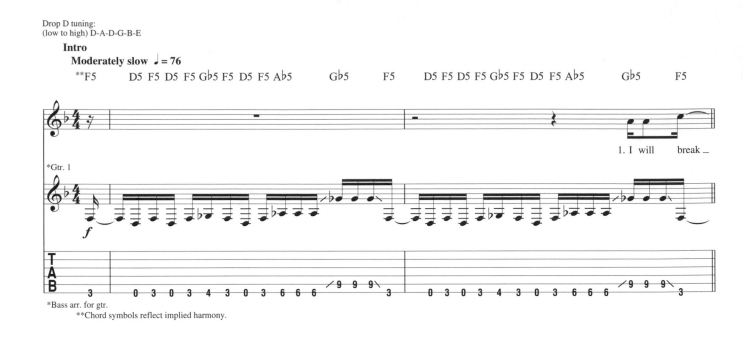

*Bass arr. for gtr.
**Chord symbols reflect implied harmony.

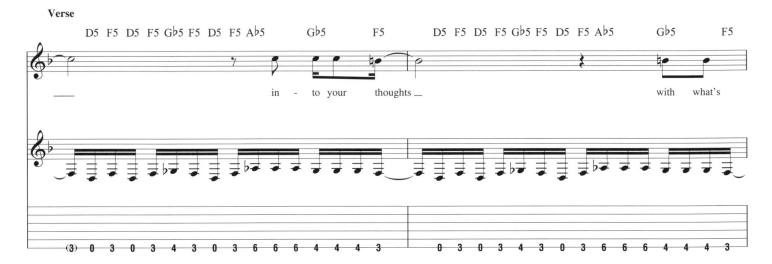

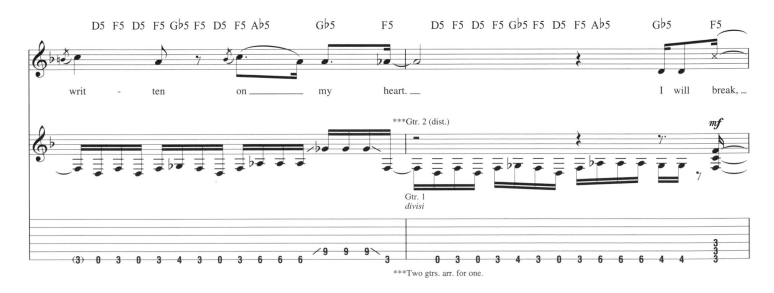

***Two gtrs. arr. for one.

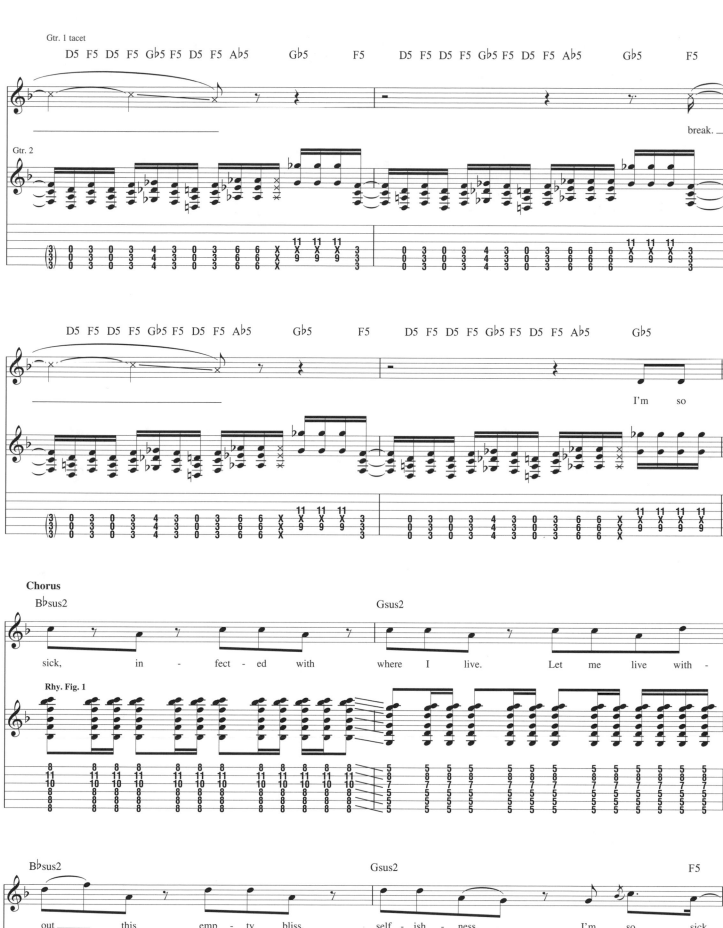

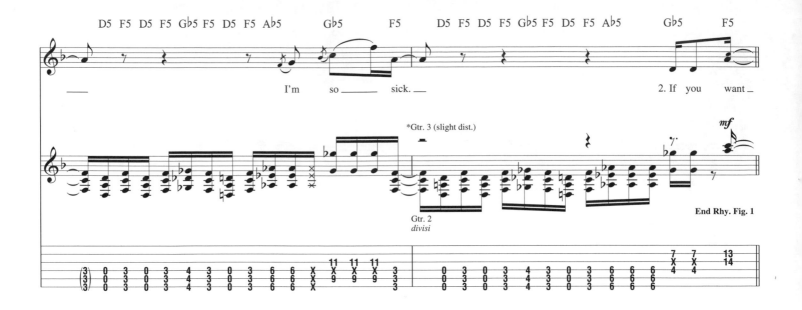

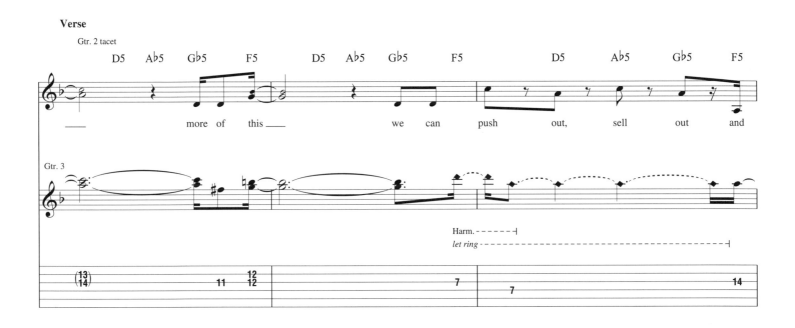

Verse

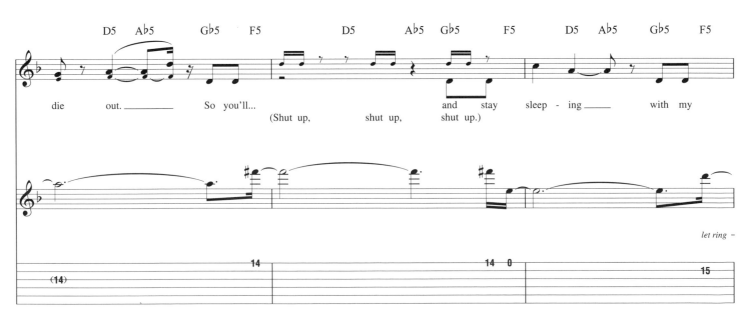

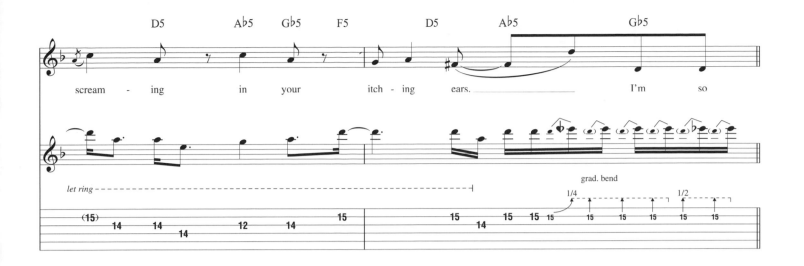

Chorus

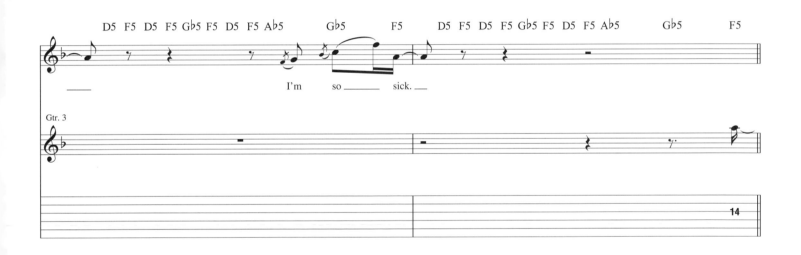

Verse

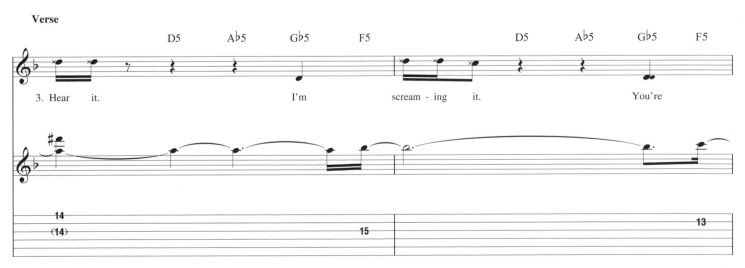

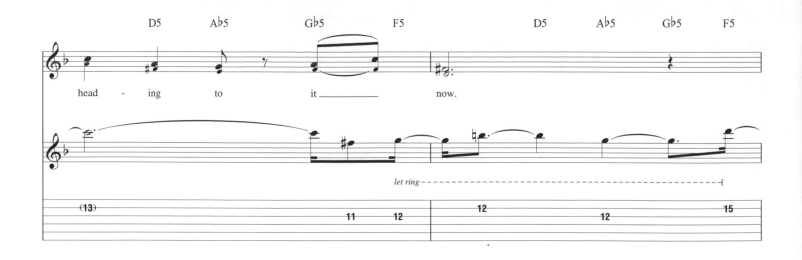

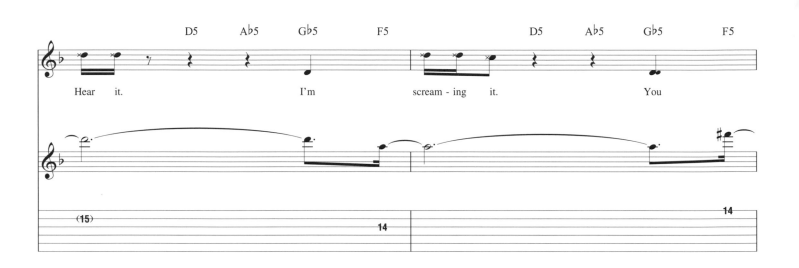

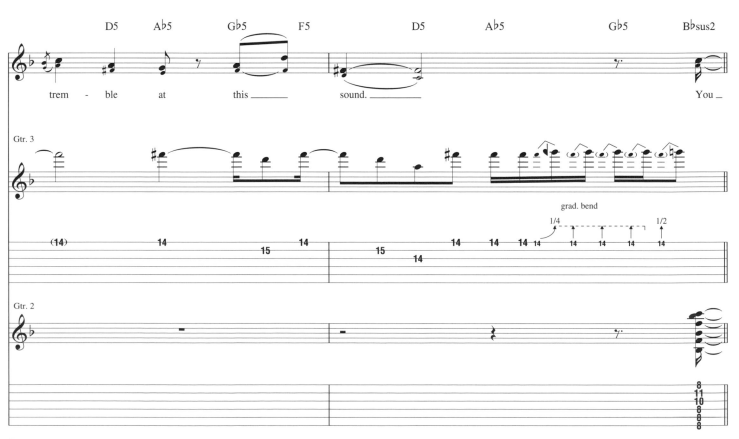

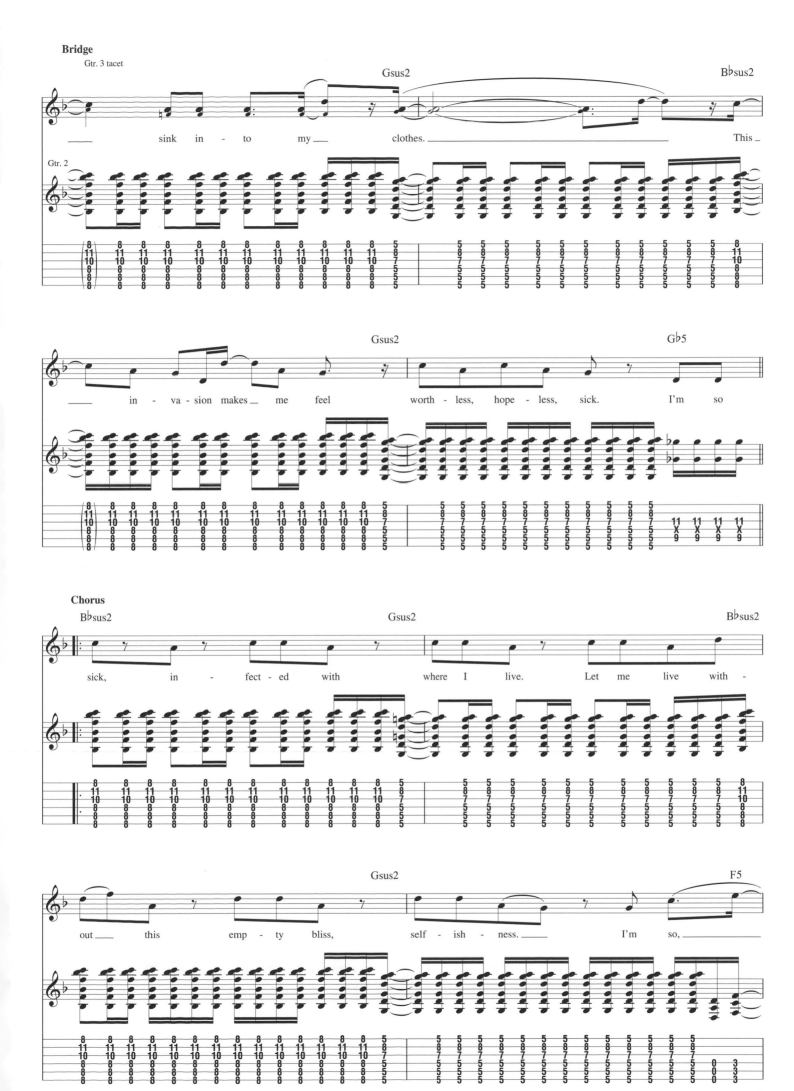

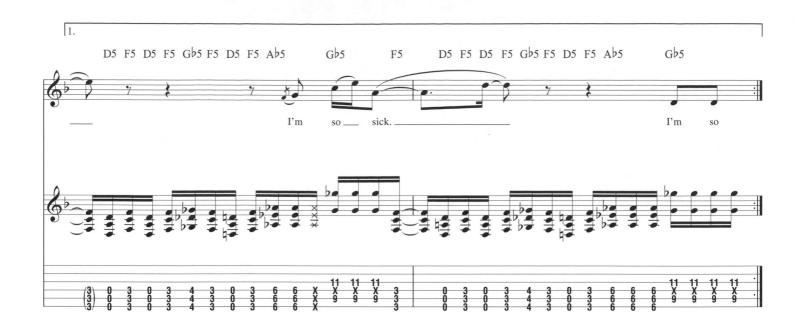

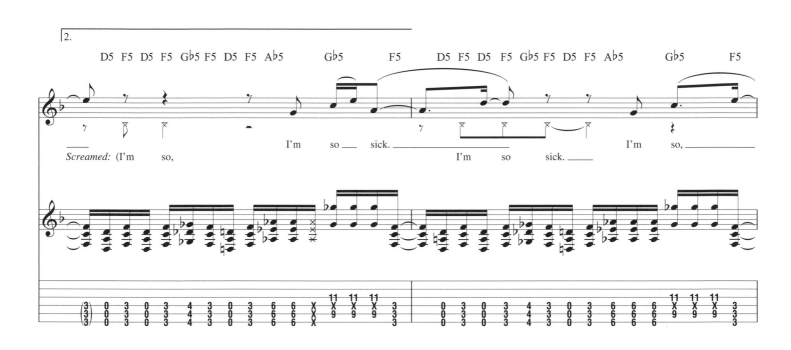

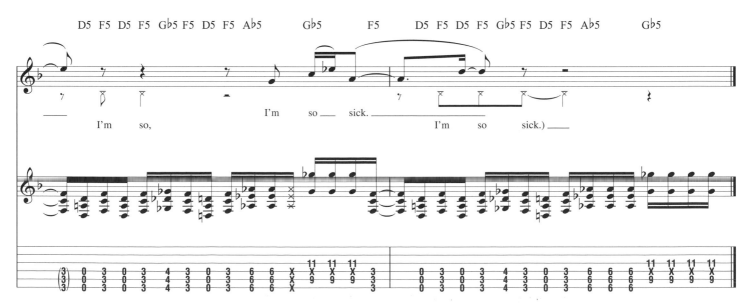

Fully Alive

Words and Music by Sameer Bhattacharya, Jared Hartmann, Kirkpatrick Seals, James Culpepper and Lacey Mosley

Drop D tuning:
(low to high) D-A-D-G-B-E

Intro

Moderately slow ♩ = 76

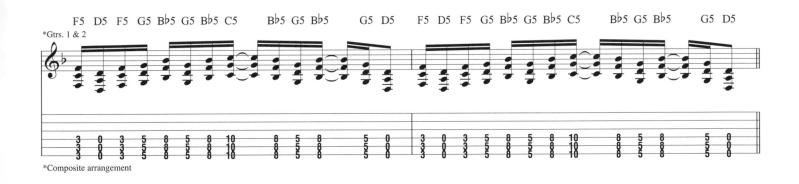

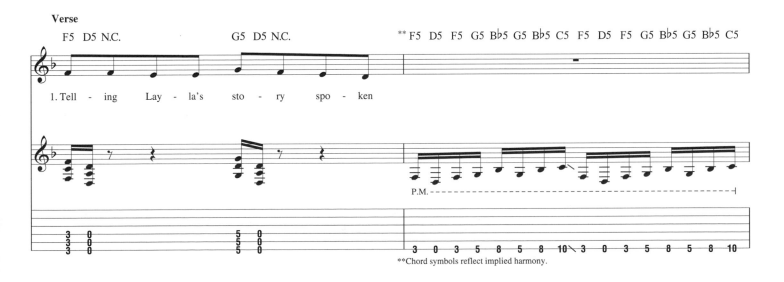

*Composite arrangement

Verse

1. Tell - ing Lay - la's sto - ry spo - ken

P.M.

**Chord symbols reflect implied harmony.

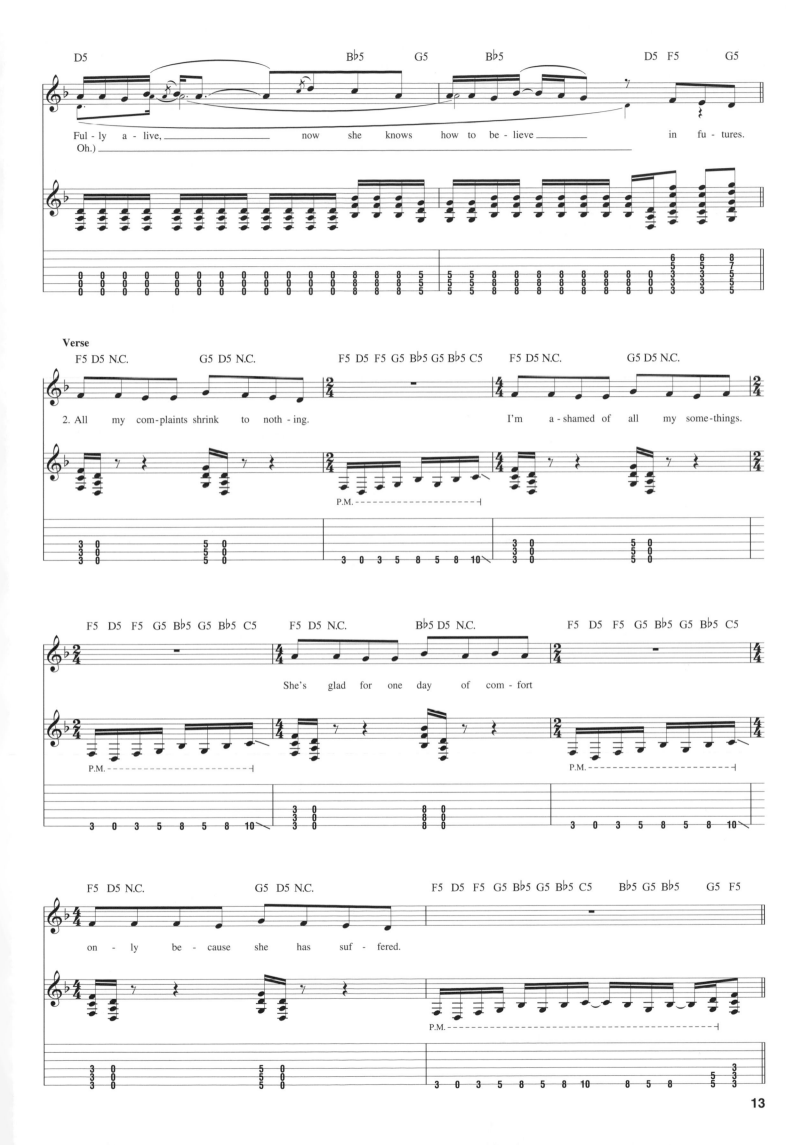

Chorus

Ful - ly a - live, _____ more than most. Read - y to smile _____ and love life.
(Oh. _____

Ful - ly a - live, _____ now she knows how to be - lieve _____ in fu - tures.
Oh.) _____

Interlude

Gtr. 2 tacet

N.C.

Gtr. 3 (dist.)

mf

w/ heavy reverb

let ring - - - - - -

Gtr. 1

mp

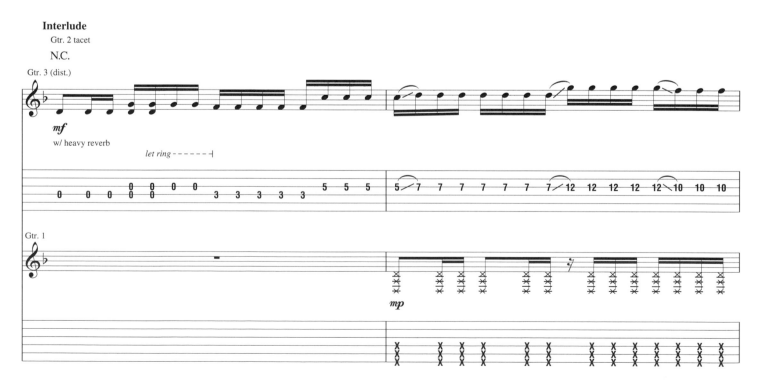

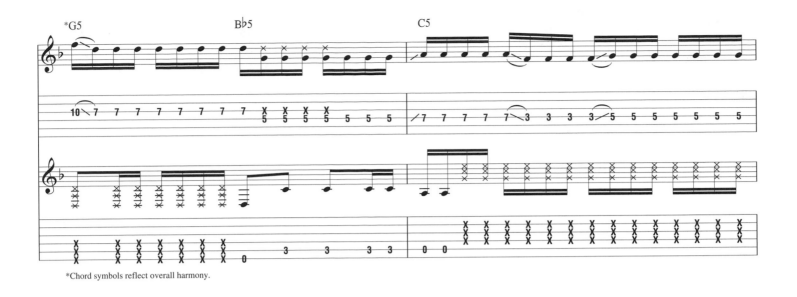

*Chord symbols reflect overall harmony.

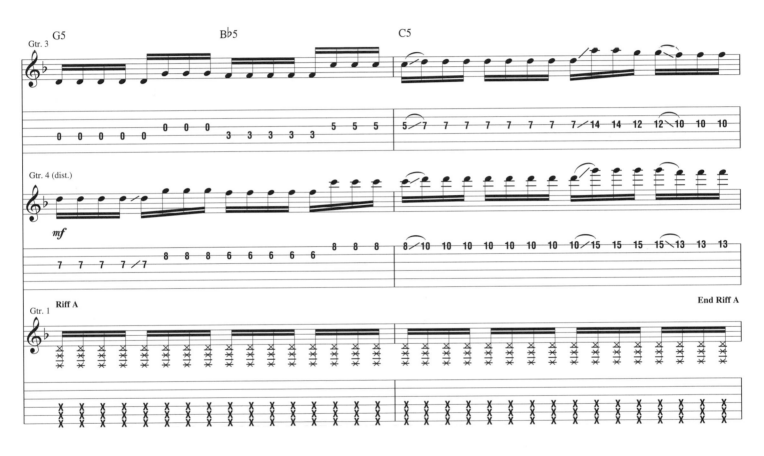

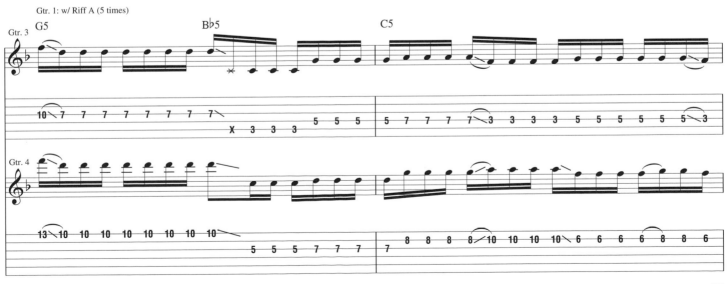

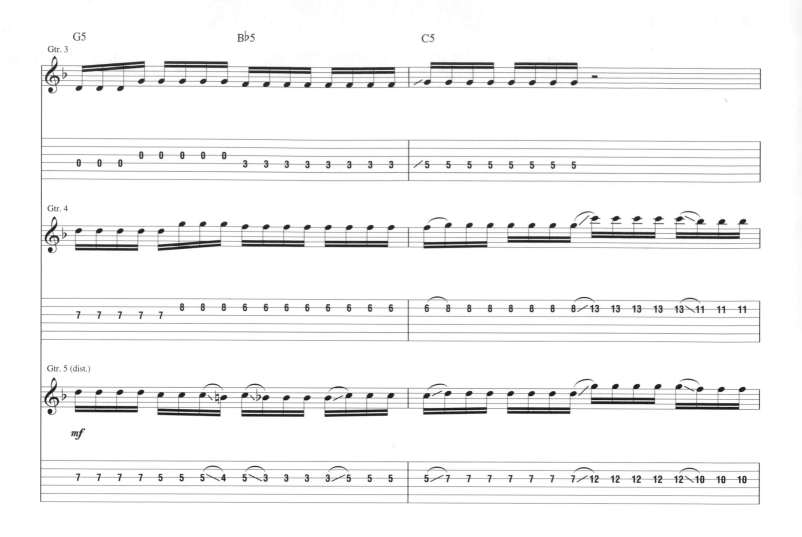

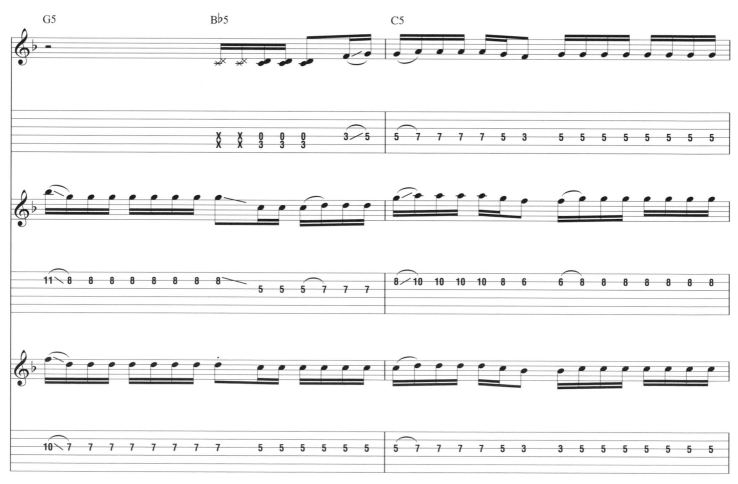

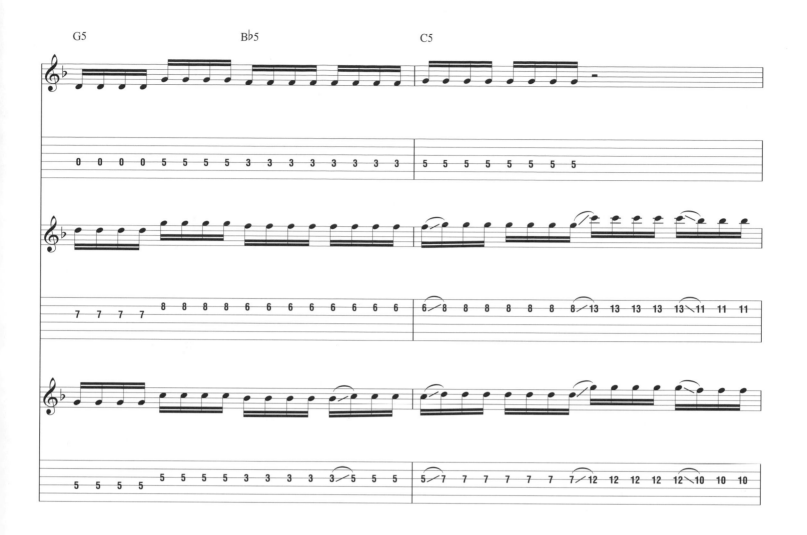

Chorus

Perfect

**Words and Music by Sameer Bhattacharya, Jared Hartmann,
Kirkpatrick Seals, James Culpepper, Lacey Mosley and Mark T. Lewis**

Drop D tuning:
(low to high) D-A-D-G-B-E

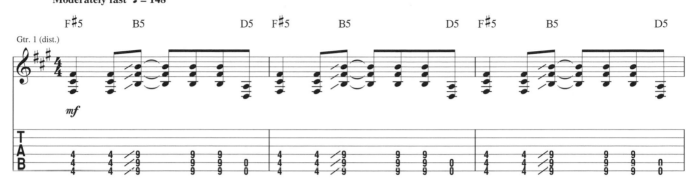

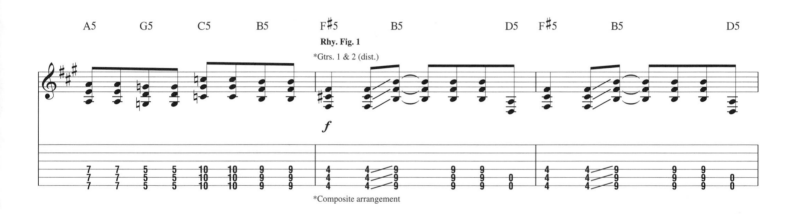

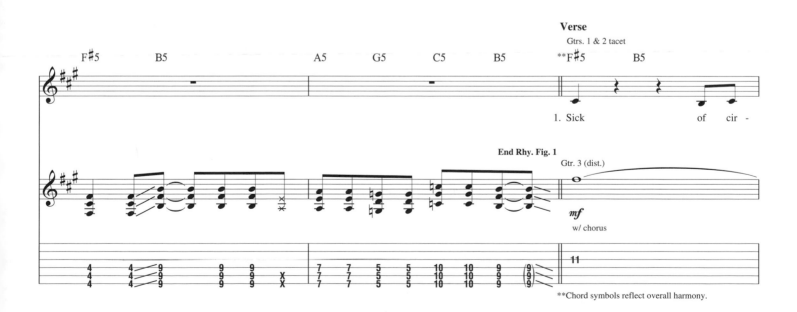

1. Sick of cir-

**Chord symbols reflect overall harmony.

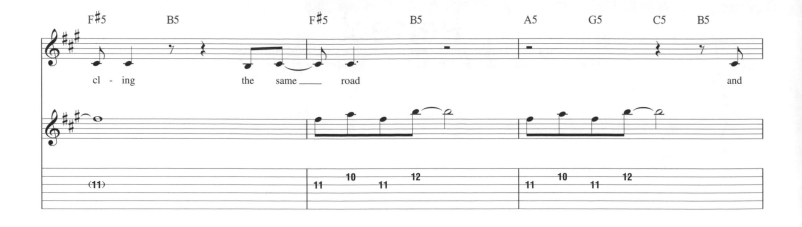

cl - ing   the same ____ road

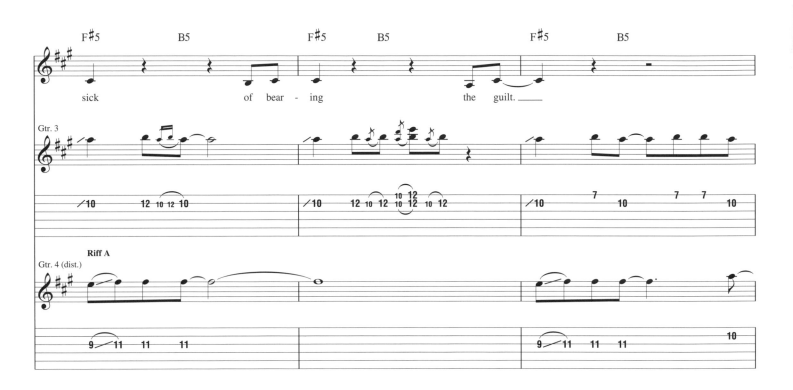

sick   of bear - ing   the guilt. ____

Riff A
Gtr. 4 (dist.)

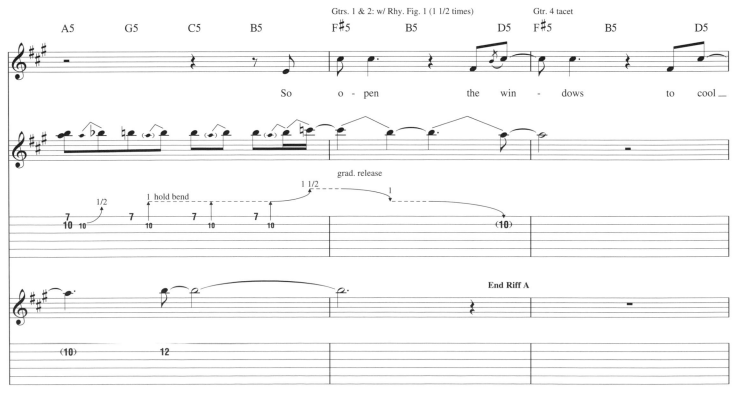

So   o - pen   the win - dows   to cool ____

End Riff A

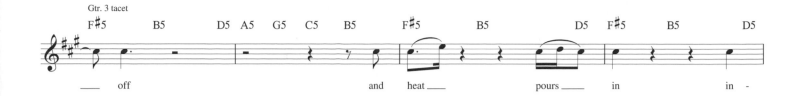

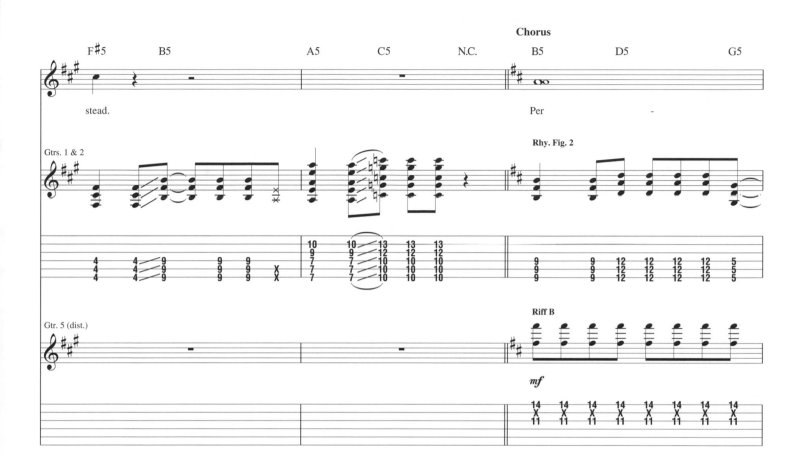

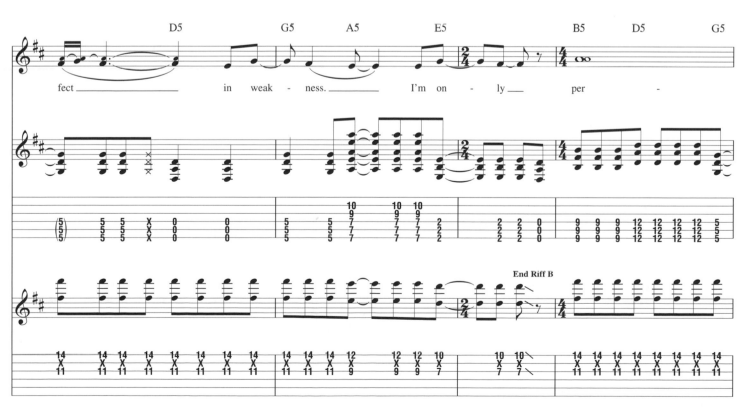

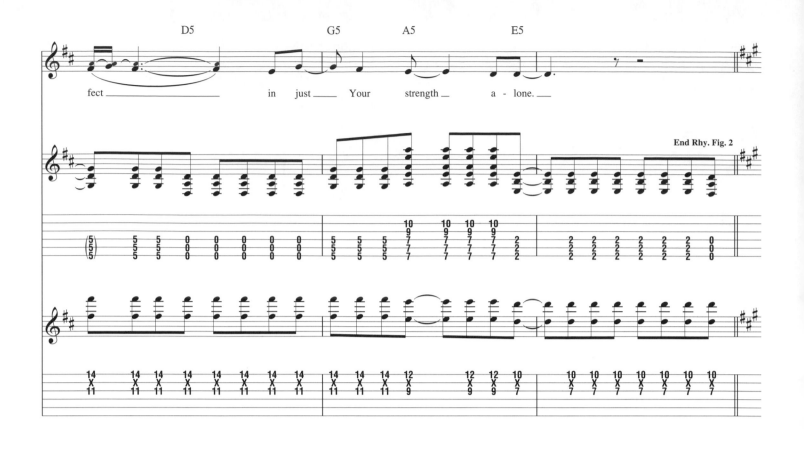

fect _____ in just ____ Your strength _____ a - lone. ____

End Rhy. Fig. 2

Verse

Gtrs. 1, 2 & 5 tacet

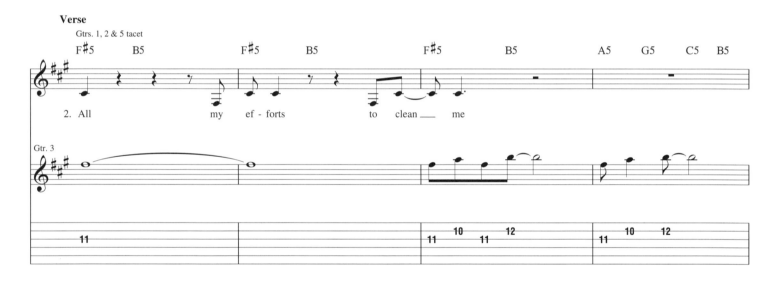

2. All my ef - forts to clean ____ me

Gtr. 3

Gtr. 4: w/ Riff A

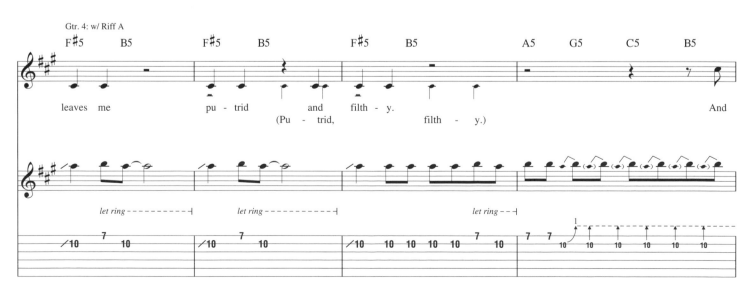

leaves me pu - trid and filth - y.

(Pu - trid, filth - y.)

And

let ring   *let ring*   *let ring*

Chorus

Gtrs. 1 & 2: w/ Rhy. Fig. 2 (1st 4 meas. 2 times)
Gtr. 5: w/ Riff B
Gtr. 6 tacet

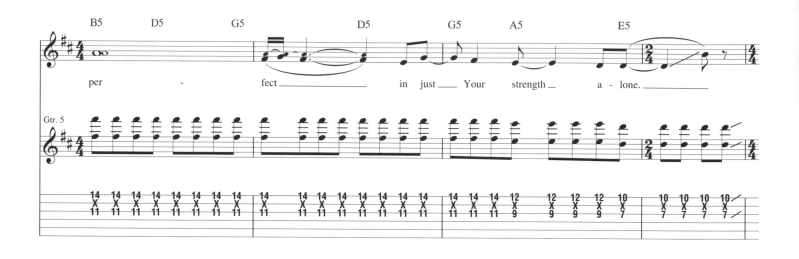

1st time, Gtrs. 1 & 2: w/ Rhy. Fig. 2
2nd time, Gtrs. 1 & 2: w/ Rhy. Fig. 2 (1st 7 meas.)

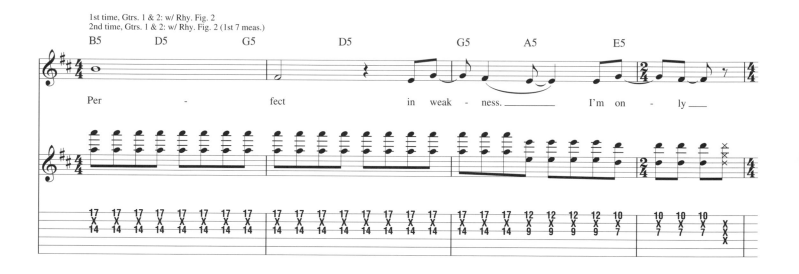

To Coda

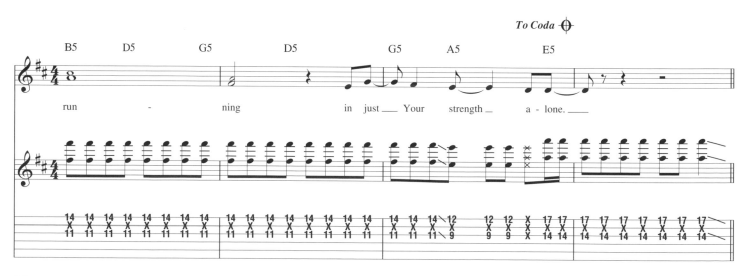

Bridge

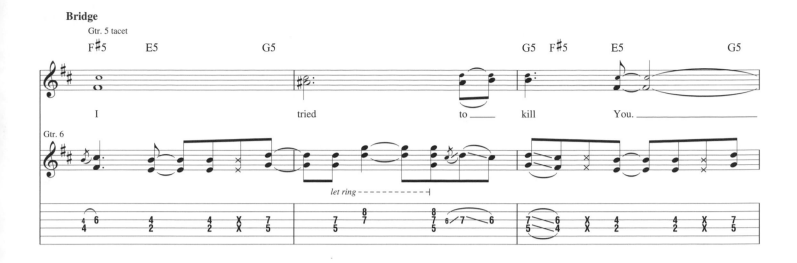

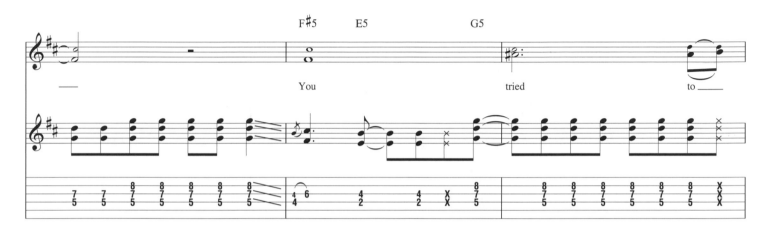

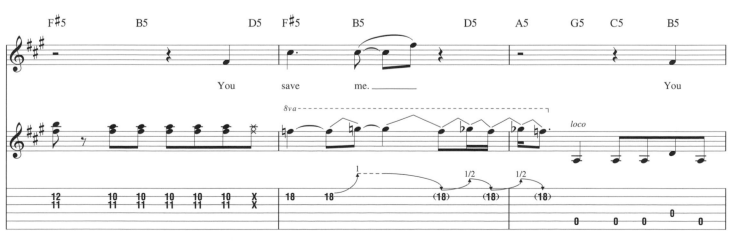

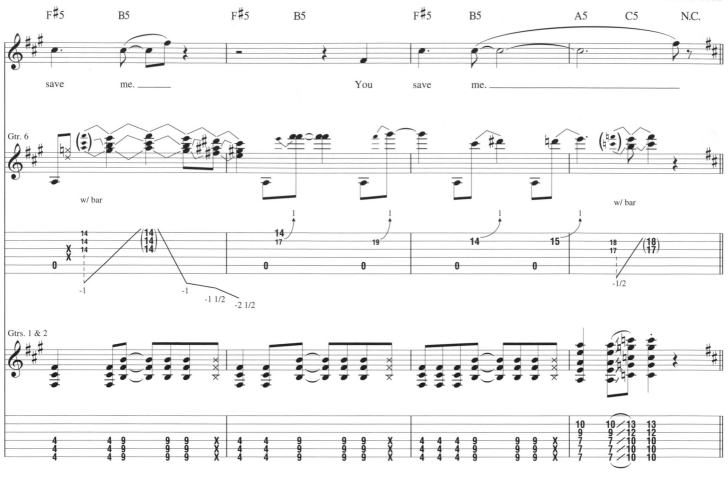

Coda

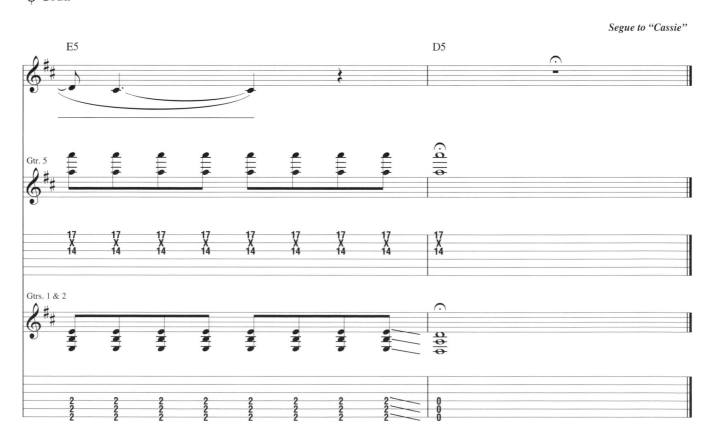

Cassie

Words and Music by Sameer Bhattacharya, Jared Hartmann, Kirkpatrick Seals, James Culpepper and Lacey Mosley

Drop D tuning:
(low to high) D-A-D-G-B-E

Intro
Fast ♩ = 168

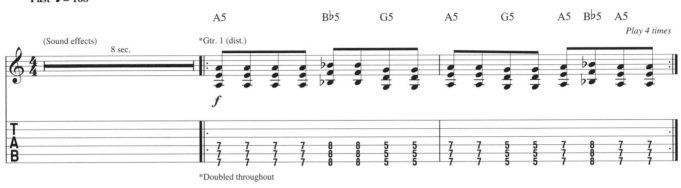

*Doubled throughout

Verse

**Bass arr. for gtr.

***Chord symbols reflect implied harmony.

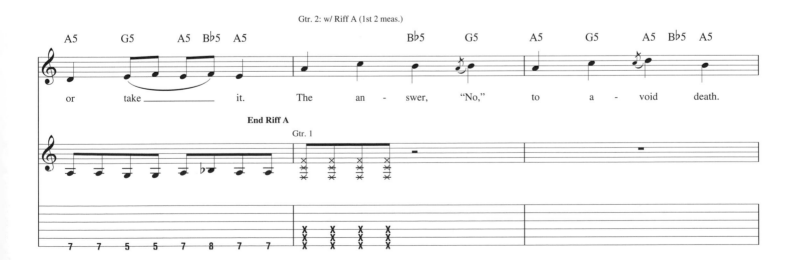

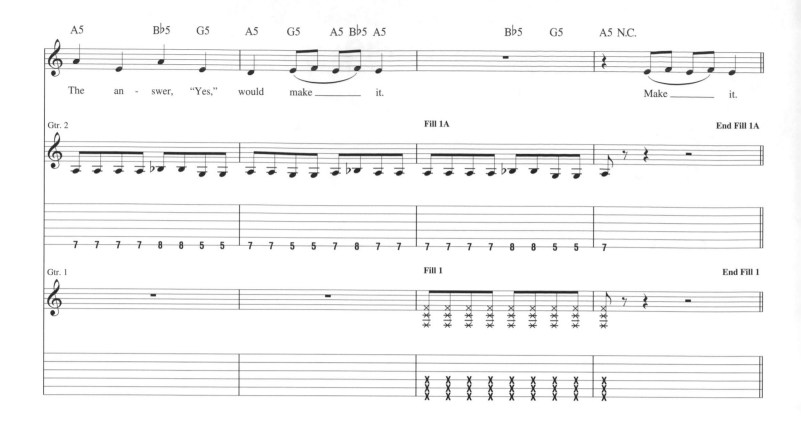

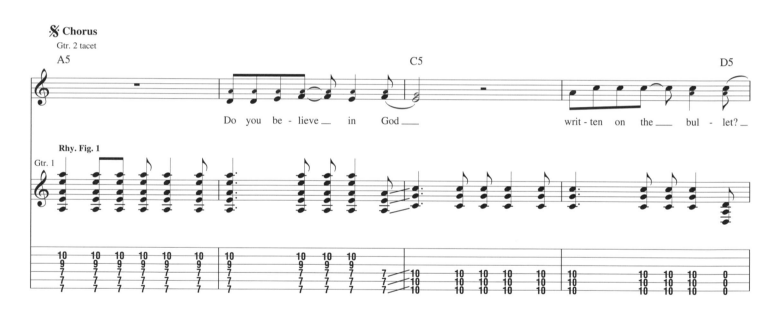

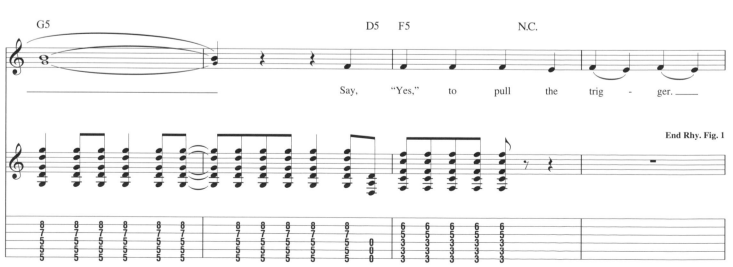

Gtr. 1: w/ Rhy. Fig. 1

Do you be - lieve ___ in God ___ writ - ten on the ___ bul - let? ___

And Cas - sie pulled the trig - ger. ___

To Coda ⊕

Interlude

Verse

Gtr. 1 tacet
Gtr. 2: w/ Riff A (2 times)

2. All heads are bowed

Gtr. 1

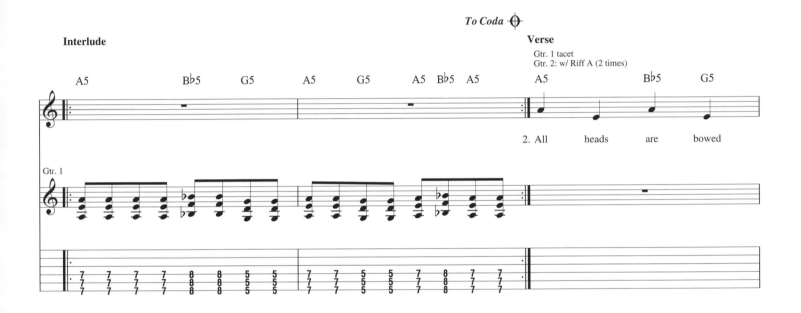

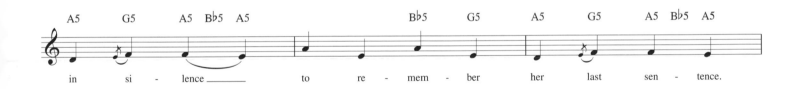

in si - lence ___ to re - mem - ber her last sen - tence.

She an - swered him know - ing what would hap - pen. Her last words still

D.S. al Coda
(take repeat)

Gtrs. 1 & 2: w/ Fills 1 & 1A

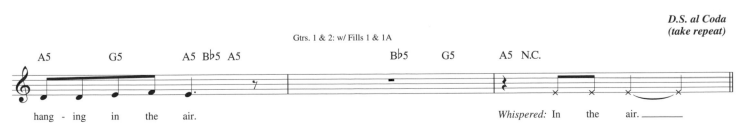

hang - ing in the air. *Whispered:* In the air. ___

29

⊕ Coda

Bridge
Half-time feel

Gtr. 1 tacet

How _____ man - y   will

Gtr. 3 (dist.)

mf

w/ flanger

Gtr. 4 (dist.)

*p ◁ *mp*   ▷ *p* ◁ *mp*   ▷ *p* ◁ *mp*   ▷ *p* ◁ *mp* ▷ *p* ◁ *mp* ▷ *p*

let ring

*Vol. swells

die? _____   Oh. _____

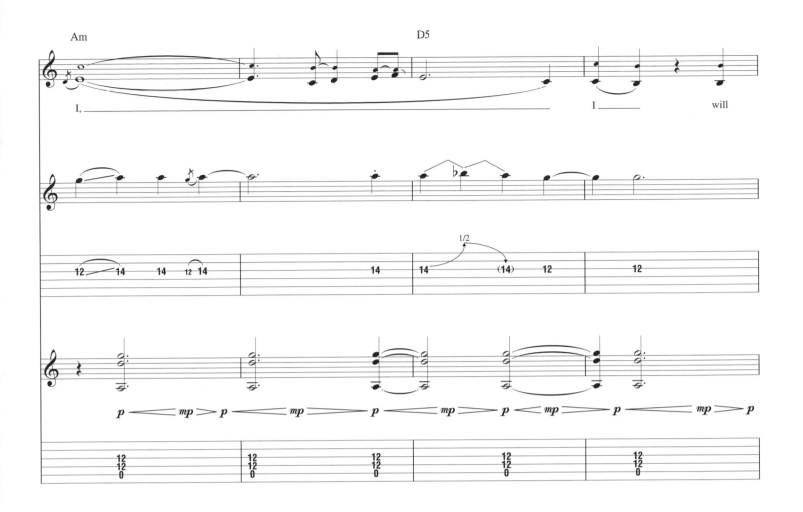

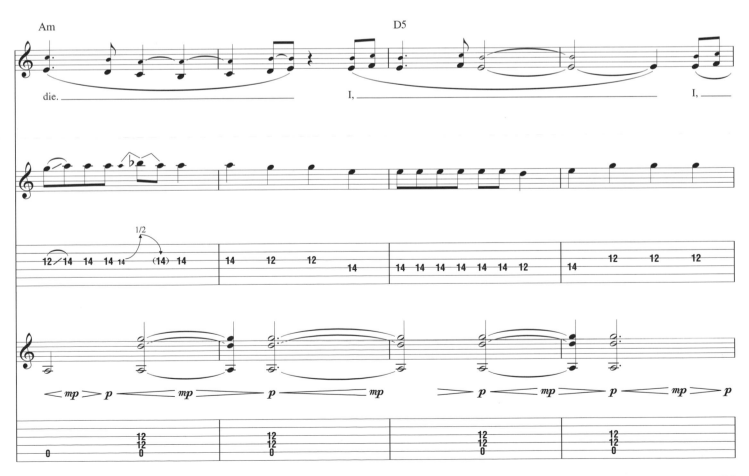

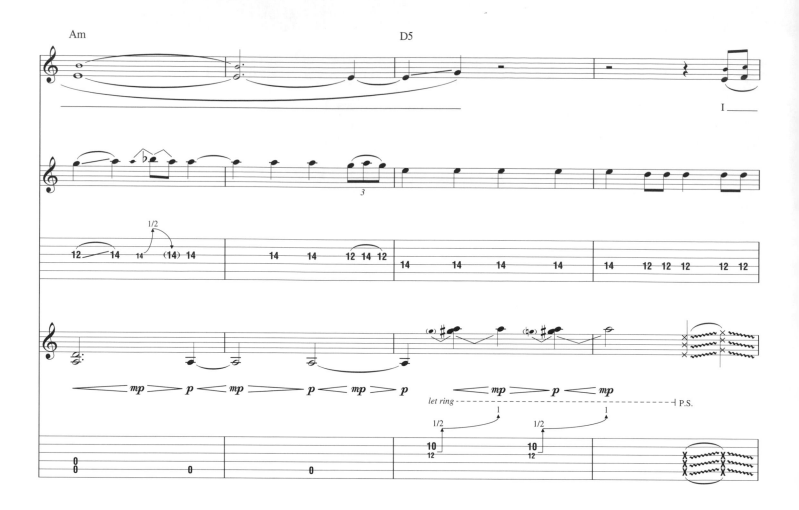

End half-time feel

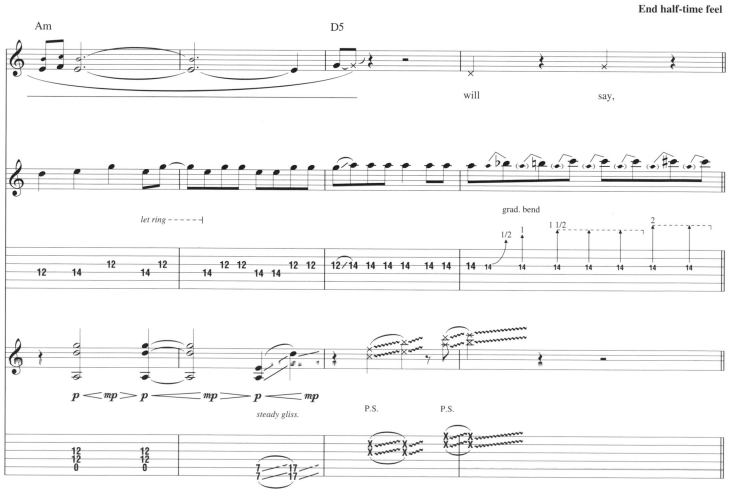

Sorrow

Words and Music by Sameer Bhattacharya, Jared Hartmann, Kirkpatrick Seals, James Culpepper and Lacey Mosley

Drop D tuning:
(low to high) D-A-D-G-B-E

Intro
Moderately ♩ = 140

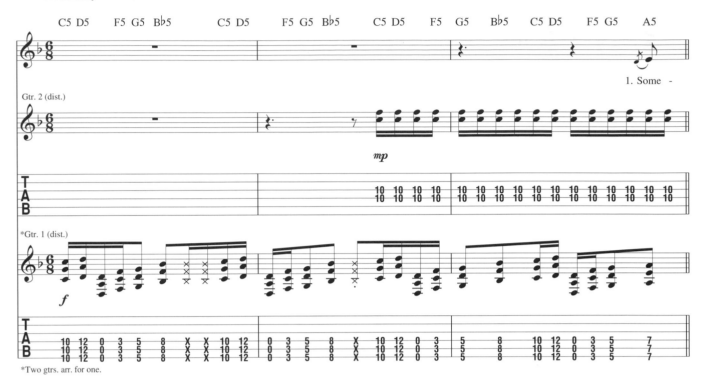

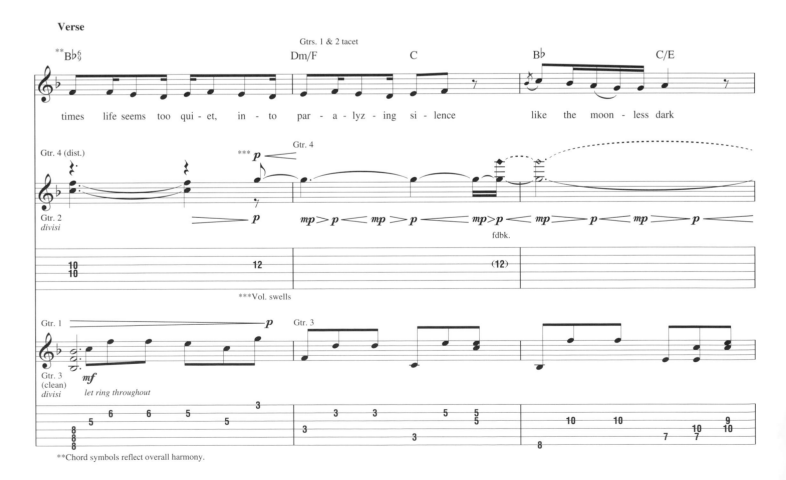

*Two gtrs. arr. for one.

Verse

*Chord symbols reflect overall harmony.

meant to make me ___ strong. Fa - mil - iar breath of my old ___ lies ___

*Vol. swell

changed the col - or in my ___ eyes. Soon He will per - fo - rate the

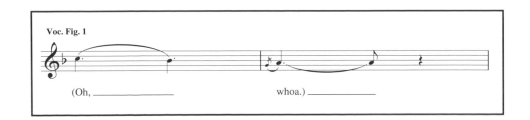

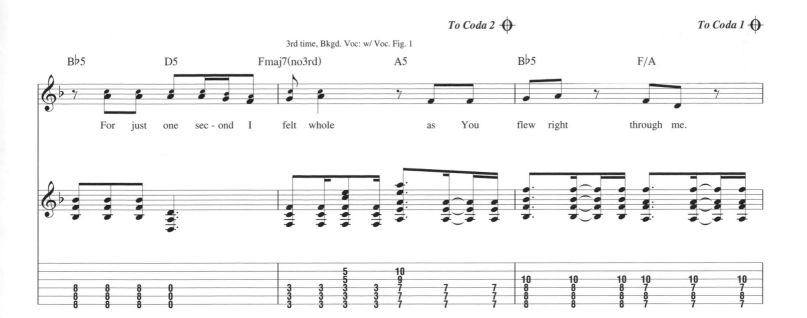

For just one sec-ond I felt whole as You flew right through me.

Verse

Gtr. 1 tacet

2. Left a-lone with on-ly re-flec-tions of the mem-'ry to

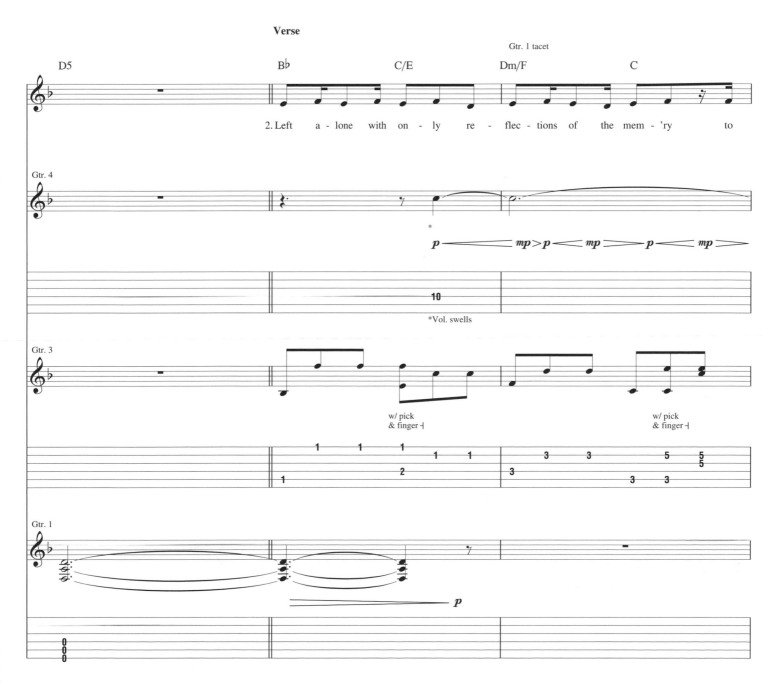

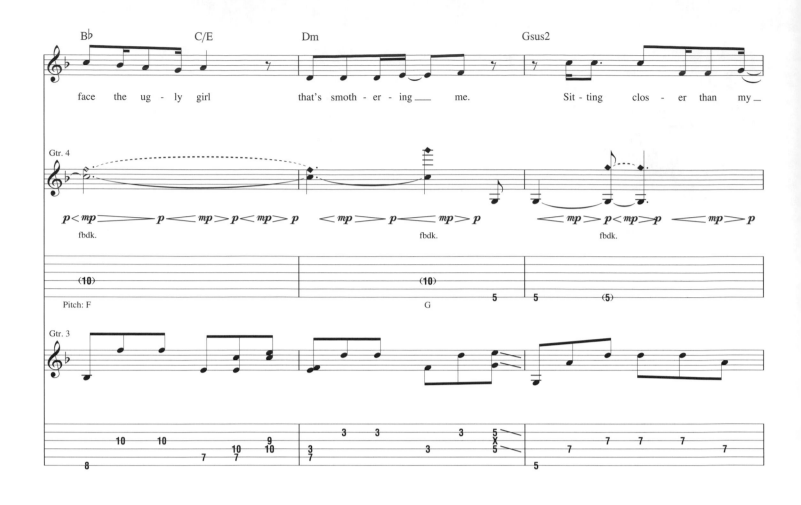

face the ug-ly girl that's smoth-er-ing____ me. Sit-ting clos-er than my____

____ pain, He knew each tear be - fore it came.

Soon He will per - fo - rate the fab - ric of the peace - ful by and by. ___ Sor - row

Coda 1

Bridge

And we kiss each __ oth - er one more __ time and

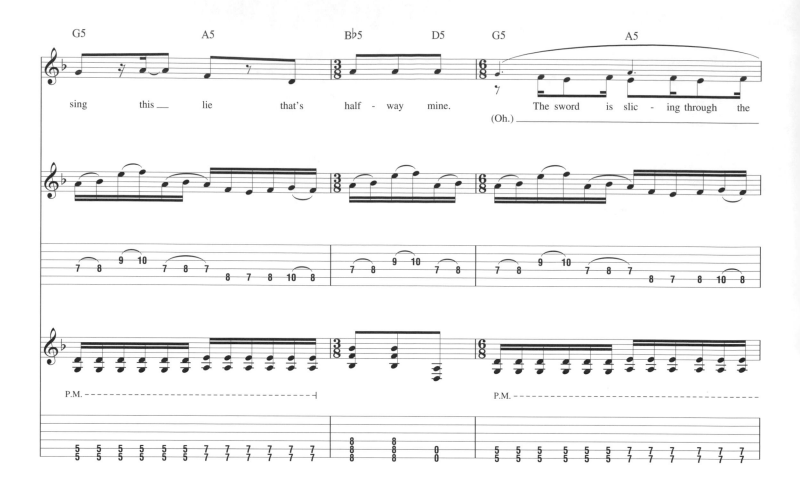

sing this __ lie that's half - way mine. The sword is slic - ing through the
(Oh.) __

D.S. al Coda 2

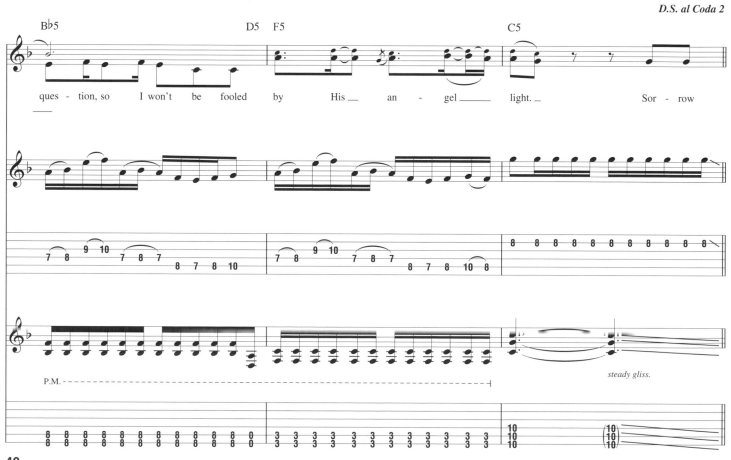

ques - tion, so I won't be fooled by His __ an - gel __ light. __ Sor - row

Coda 2

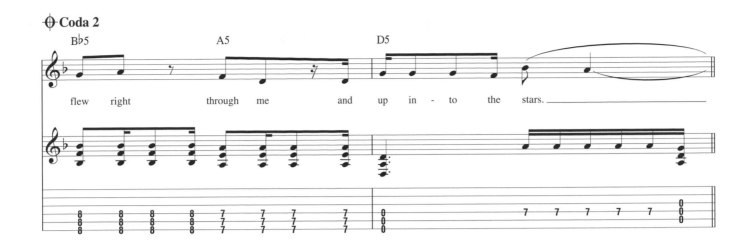

flew right   through me   and up in - to the stars.

Outro

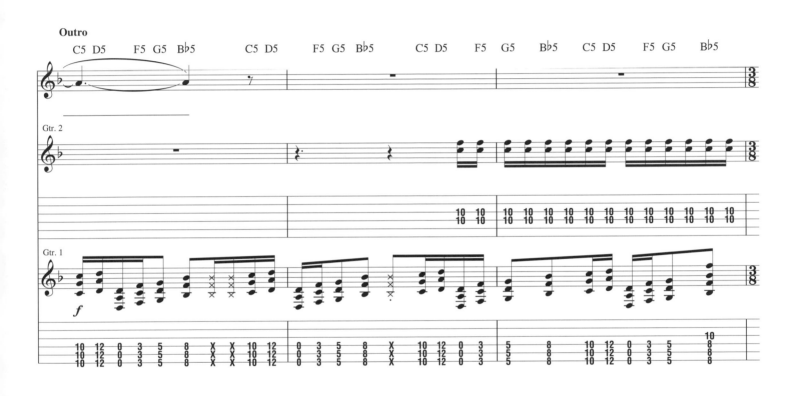

Screamed: Joy   will   come.

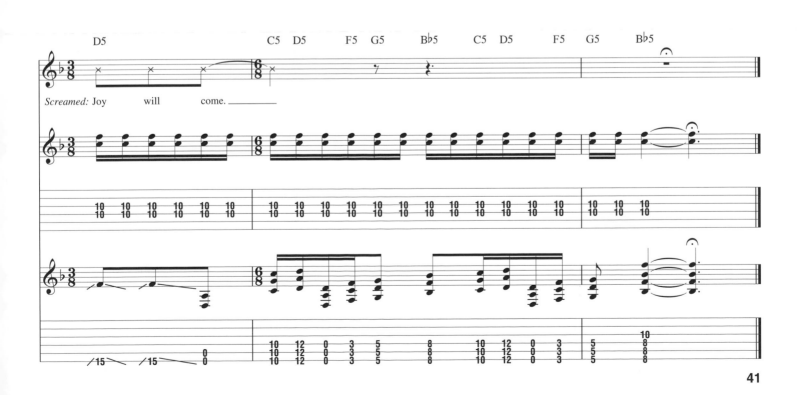

I'm Sorry

Words and Music by Sameer Bhattacharya, Jared Hartmann, Kirkpatrick Seals, James Culpepper and Lacey Mosley

Drop D tuning:
(low to high) D-A-D-G-B-E

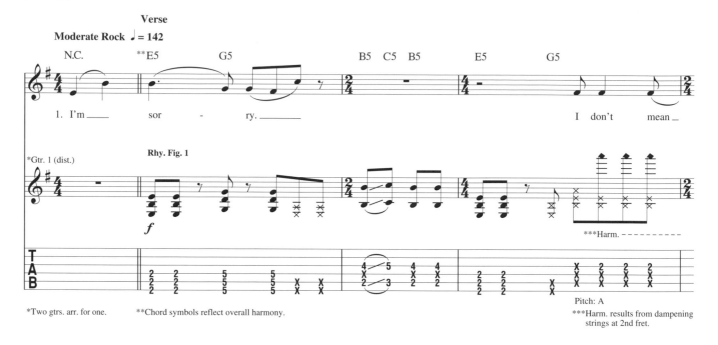

*Two gtrs. arr. for one.   **Chord symbols reflect overall harmony.

***Harm. results from dampening strings at 2nd fret.

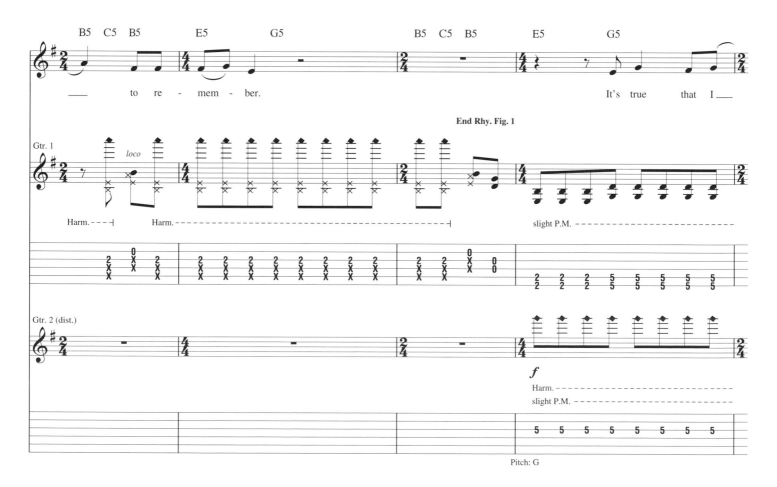

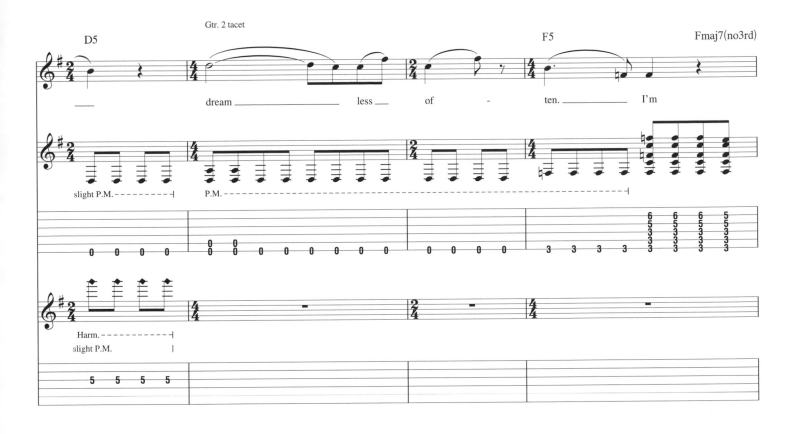

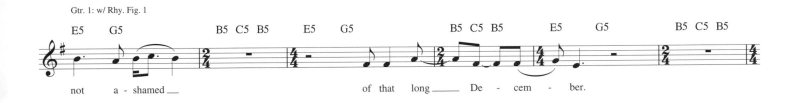

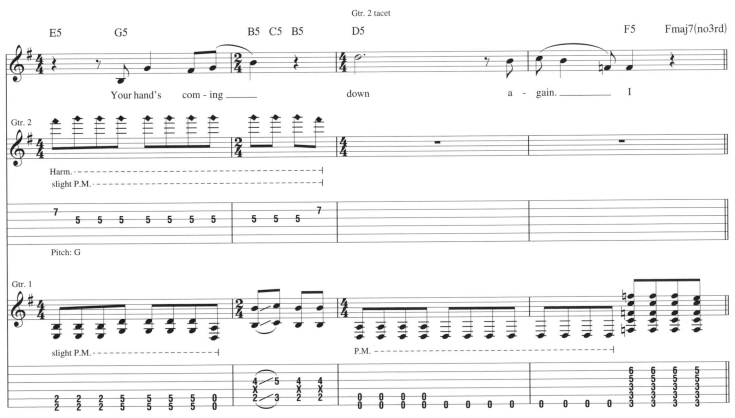

3rd time, Gtrs. 4 & 5 tacet

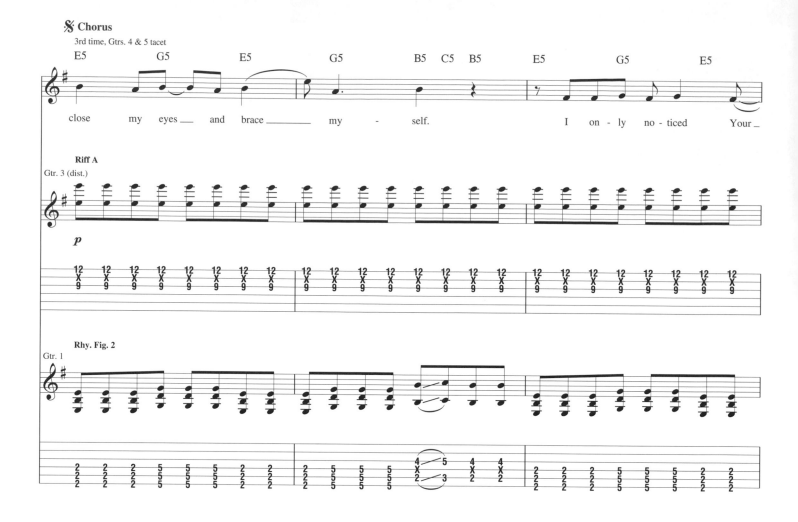

close my eyes ___ and brace ___ my - self. I on - ly no - ticed Your ___

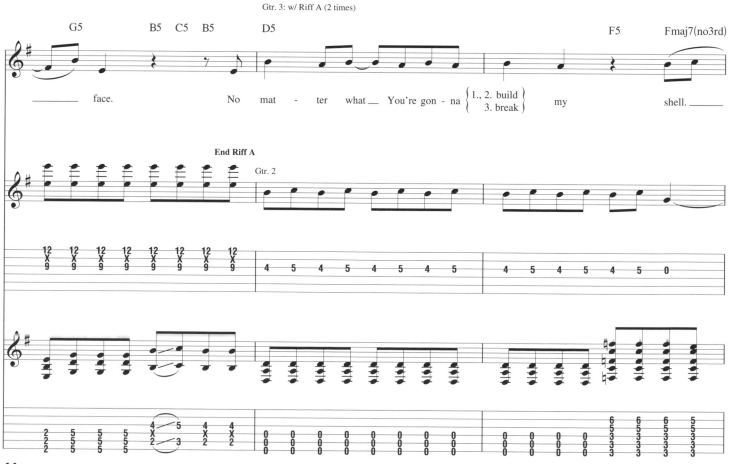

Gtr. 3: w/ Riff A (2 times)

___ face. No mat - ter what ___ You're gon - na {1., 2. build / 3. break} my shell. ___

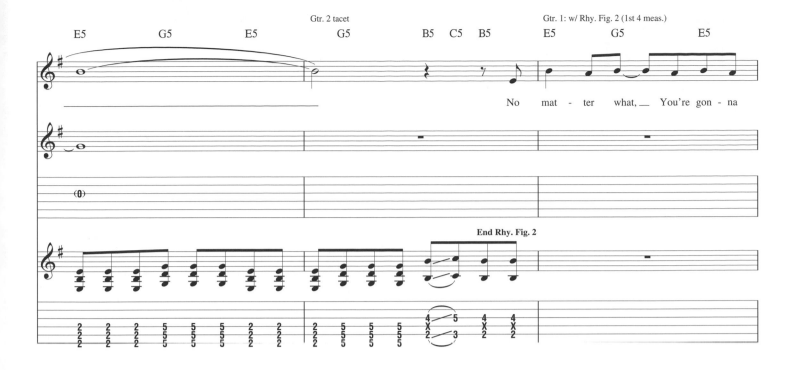

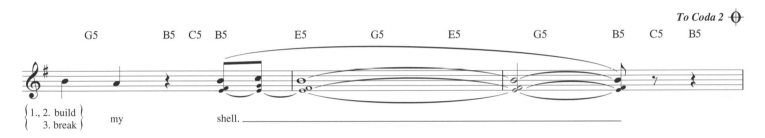

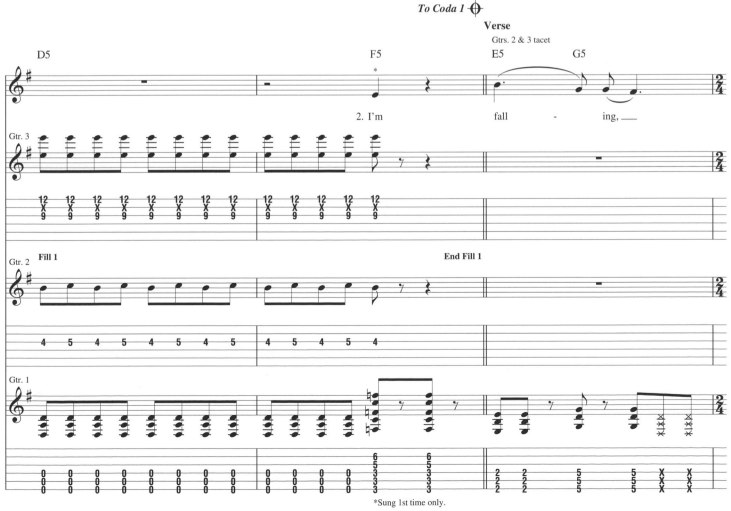

*Sung 1st time only.

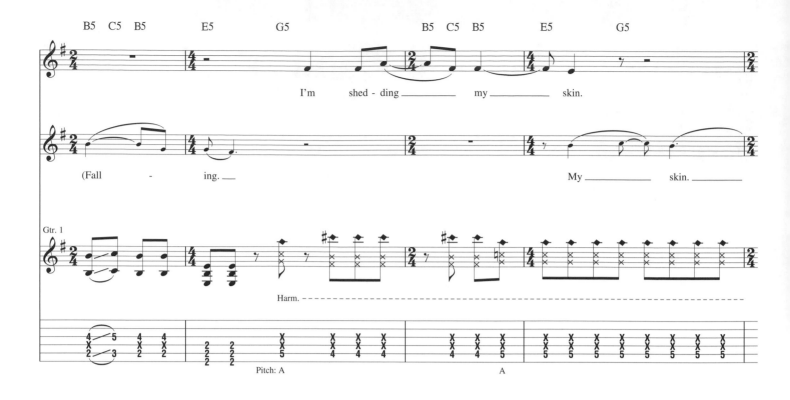

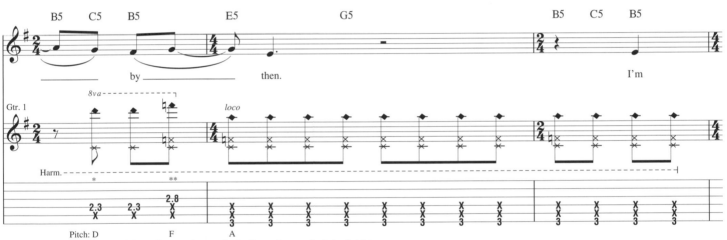

*Harmonic located approx. three-tenths the distance between the 2nd to 3rd frets.

**Approx. eight-tenths.

D.S. al Coda 1

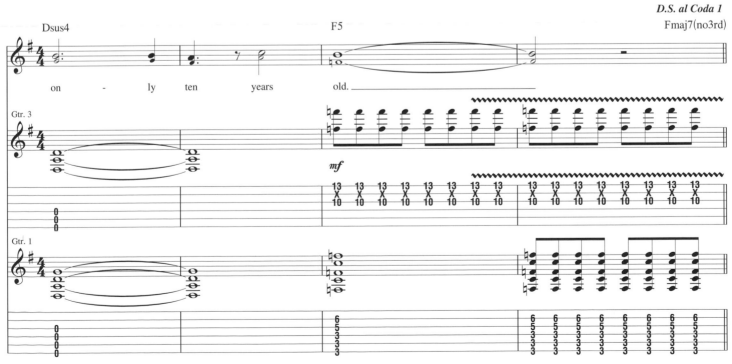

⊕ Coda 1

Gtrs. 1, 2 & 3 tacet

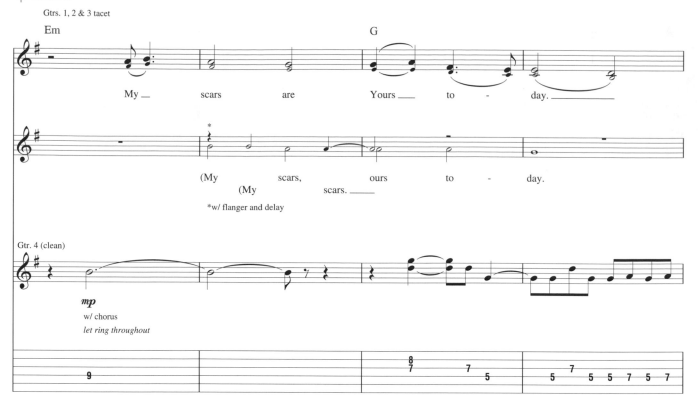

My __ scars are Yours __ to - day. __

(My scars, ours to - day.
(My scars. __

*w/ flanger and delay

Gtr. 4 (clean)

mp
w/ chorus
let ring throughout

This sto - ry __ ends so good. __

Day. __

Gtr. 5 (slight dist.)

mp
w/ chorus
let ring

let ring

Gtr. 4

D.S. al Coda 2

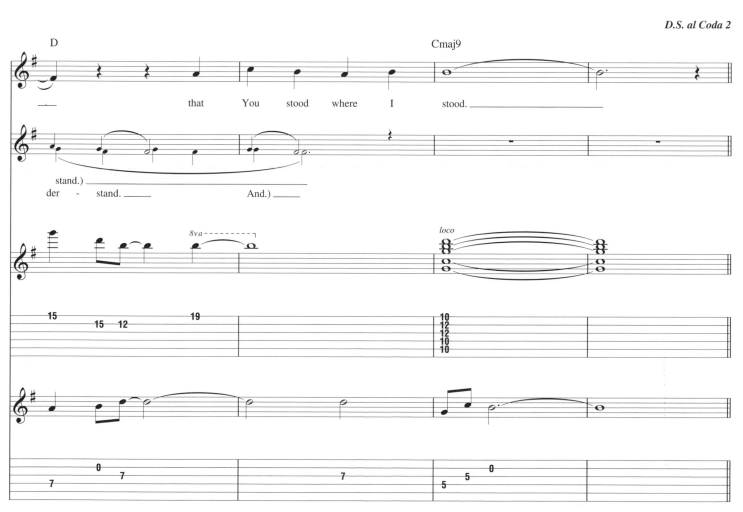

⊕ Coda 2

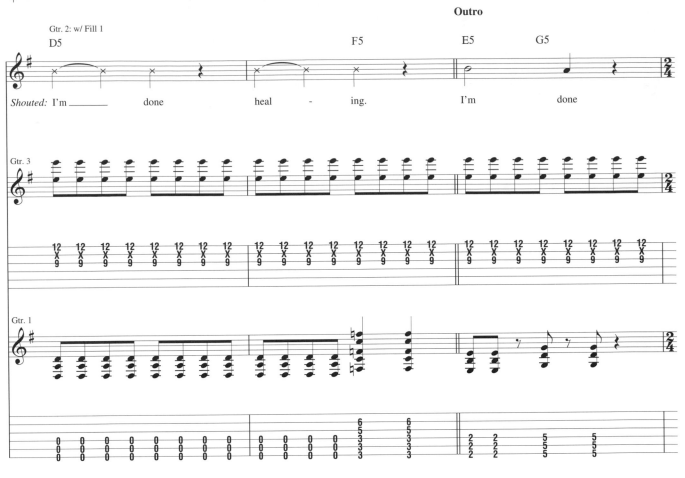

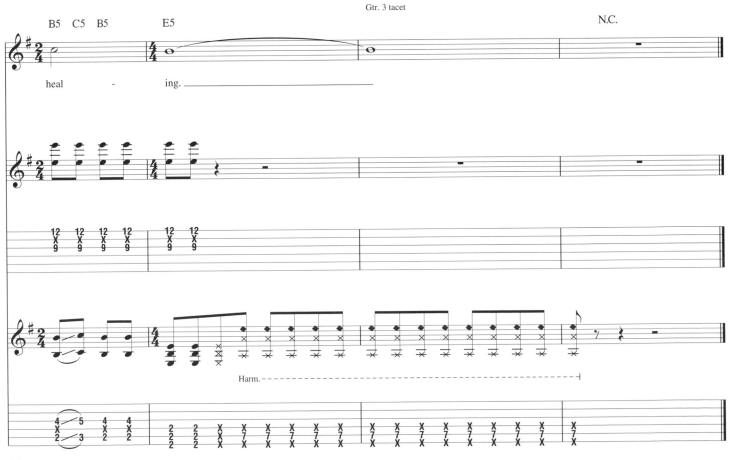

All Around Me

Words and Music by Sameer Bhattacharya, Jared Hartmann, Kirkpatrick Seals, James Culpepper and Lacey Mosley

Drop D tuning:
(low to high) D-A-D-G-B-E

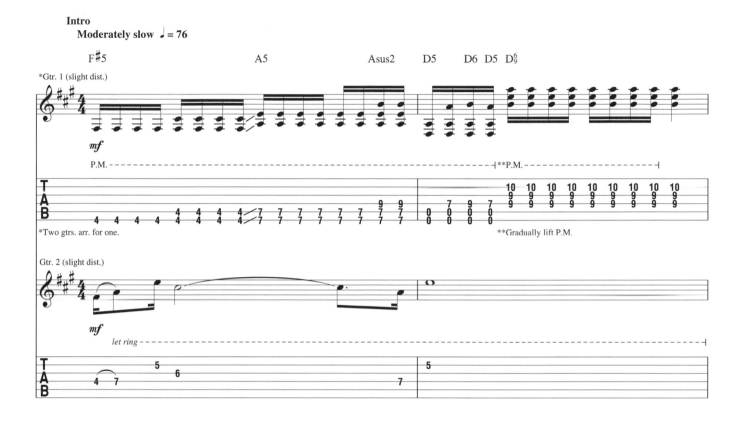

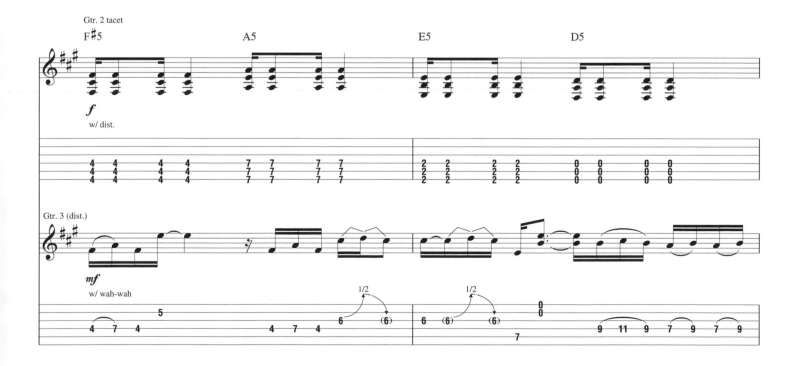

Verse

Gtr. 1 tacet

*F#m   A/E

1. My hands are search - ing for ____ You. My

Gtr. 4 (slight dist.)

mf

**w/ delay

**Set for eighth-note regeneration w/ 1 repeat.

***w/ delay

*Chord symbols reflect overall harmony.

***Set for eighth-note regeneration w/ 8 repeats.

Gtr. 3 tacet

Dmaj7   F#m   A/E

arms are out - stretched to - wards You. I feel You on ____ my fin - ger - tips. ____ My

Gtr. 4

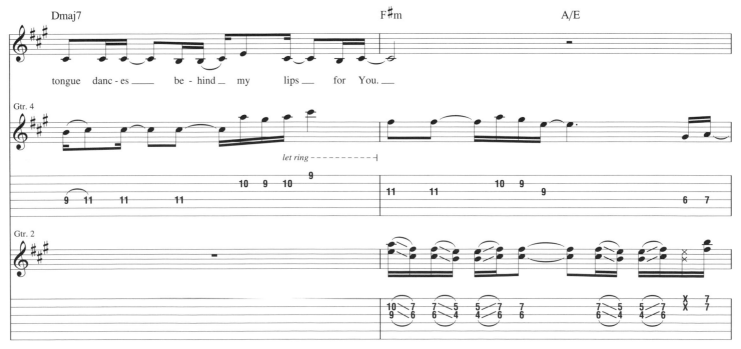

Dmaj7   F#m   A/E

tongue danc - es ____ be - hind ___ my lips ____ for You. ____

Gtr. 4

let ring

Gtr. 2

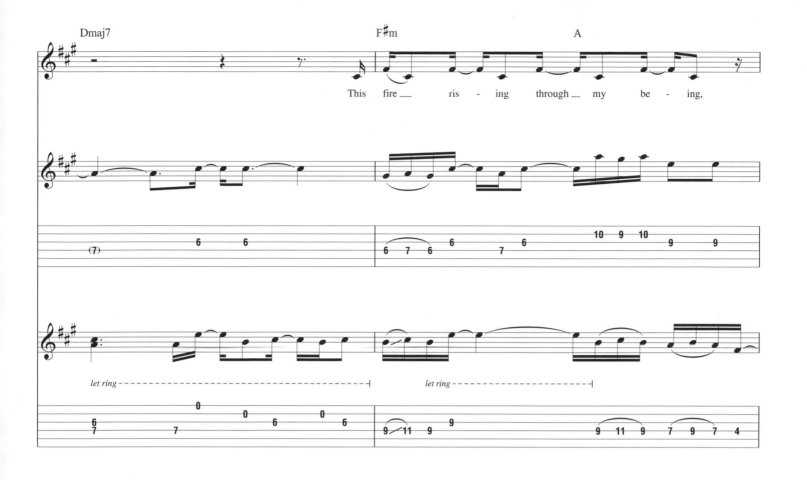

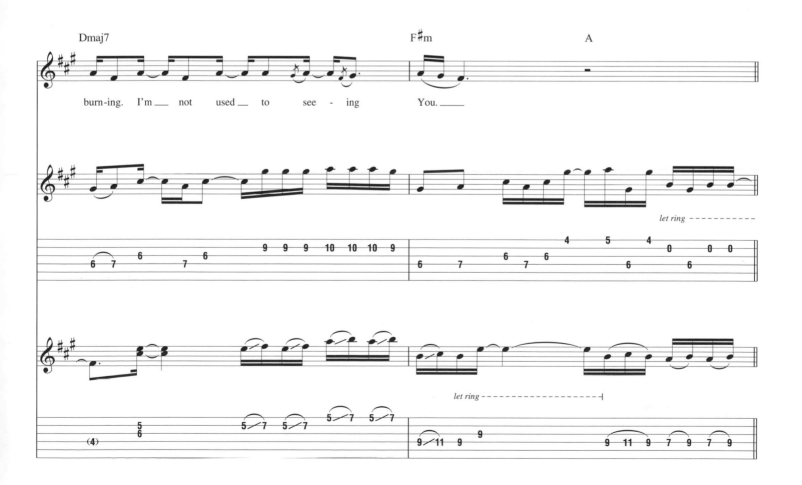

Pre-Chorus

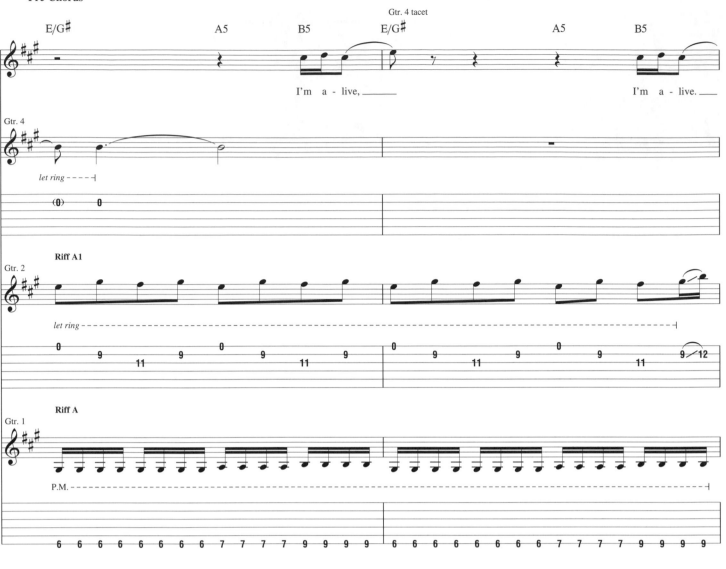

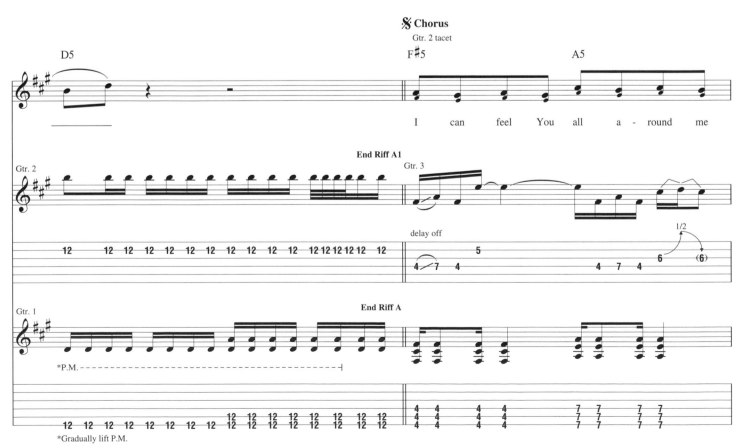

*Gradually lift P.M.

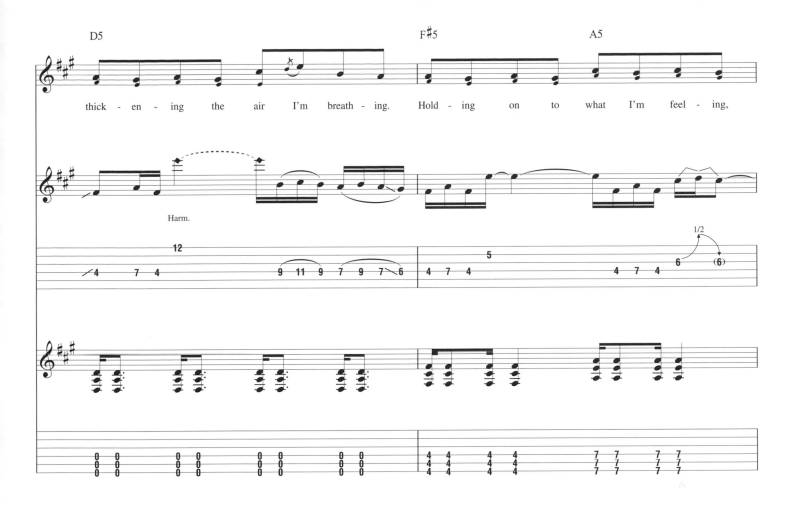

thick - en - ing the air I'm breath - ing. Hold - ing on to what I'm feel - ing,

To Coda 1 ⊕
To Coda 2 ⊕

sa - vor - ing this heart that's heal - ing.

2. My

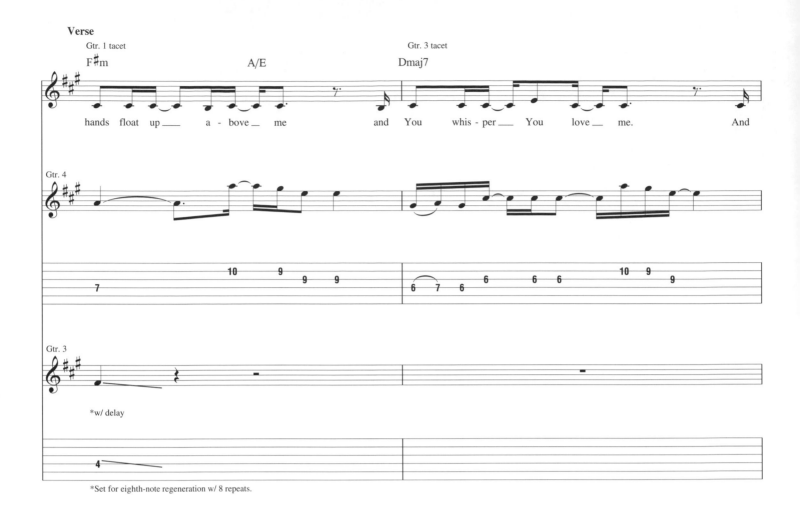

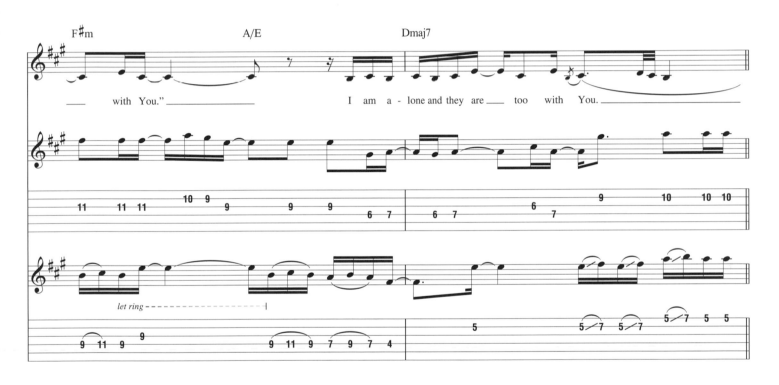

D.S. al Coda 1

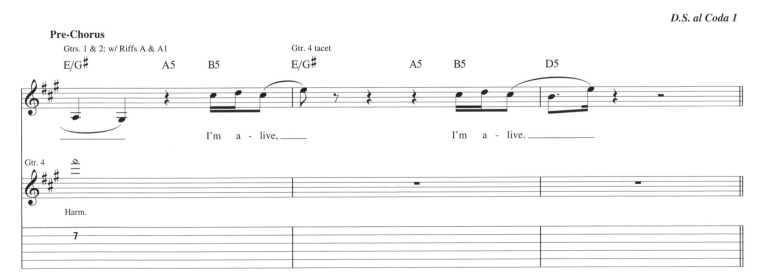

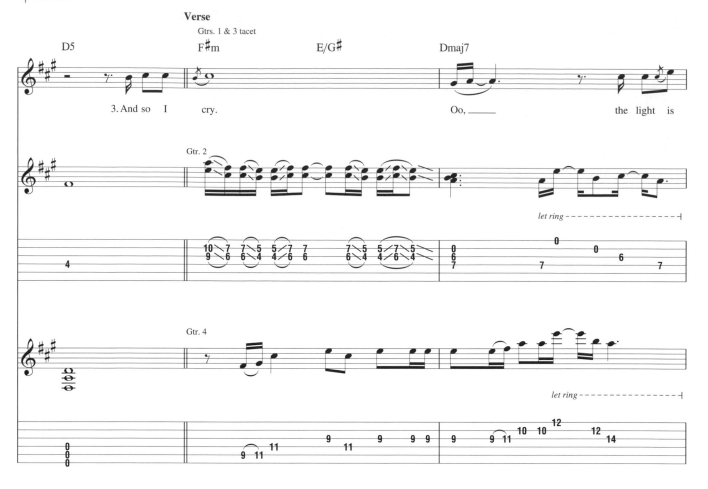

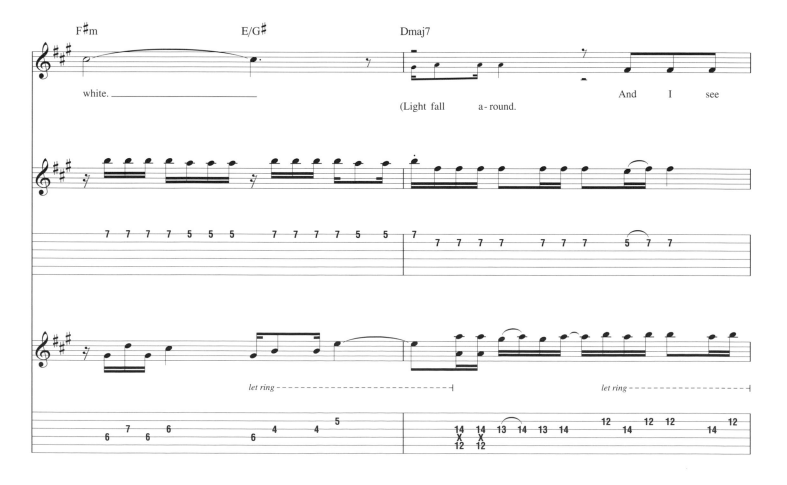

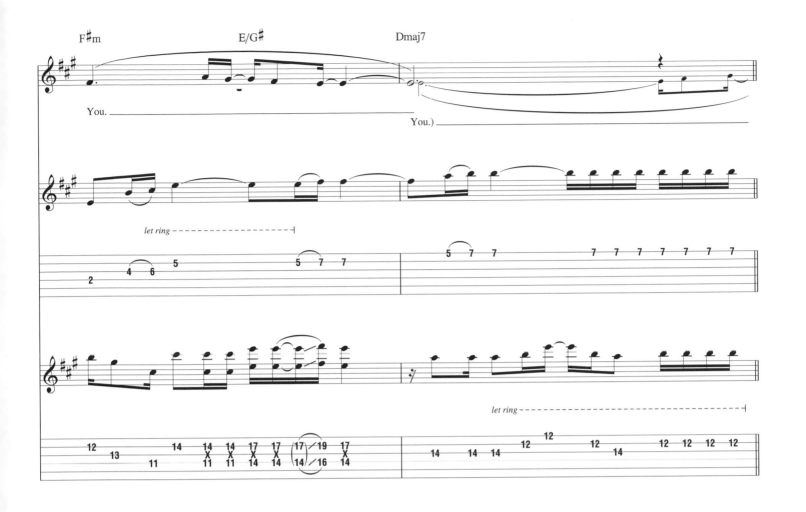

Pre-Chorus

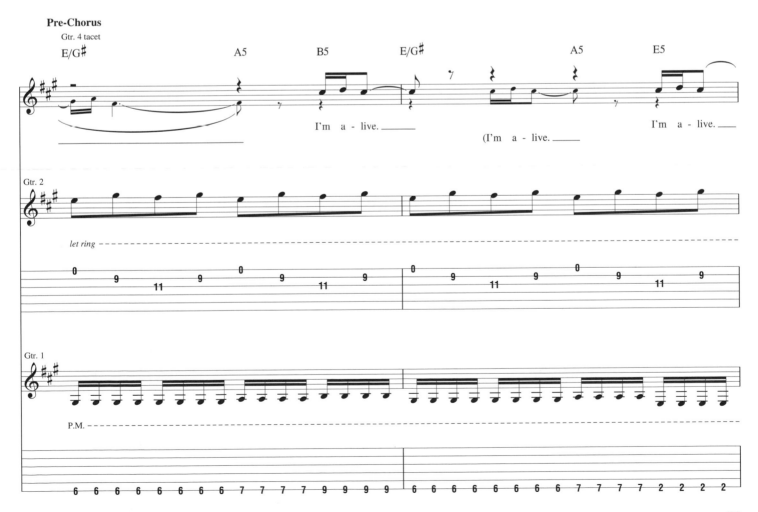

I'm a - live.)
I'm a - live.
I'm a - live.

let ring

P.M.

*P.M.

*Gradually lift P.M.

⊕ Coda 2

Outro

Double-time feel

End double-time feel

Gtr. 3 tacet

F♯5   A5   B5   D5

Take my hand, I give it to You. Now You owe me all I am. You said You would nev - er leave me. I be - lieve You. I be - lieve.

Gtr. 1

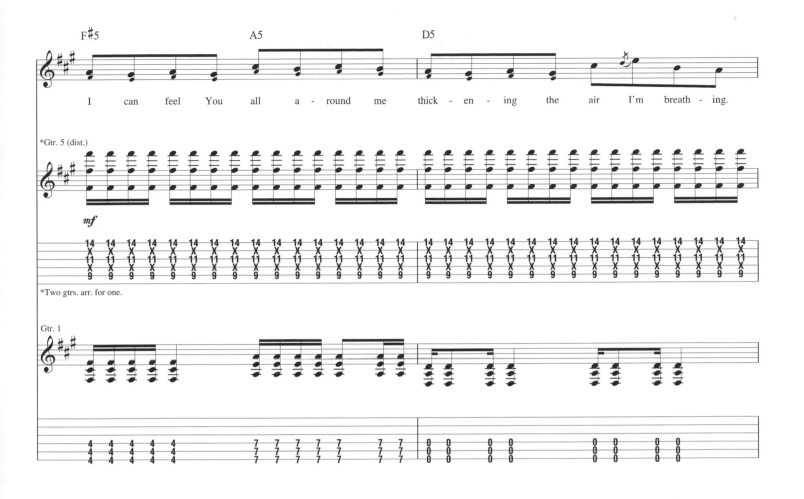

I can feel You all a - round me thick - en - ing the air I'm breath - ing.

*Gtr. 5 (dist.)

*Two gtrs. arr. for one.

Gtr. 1

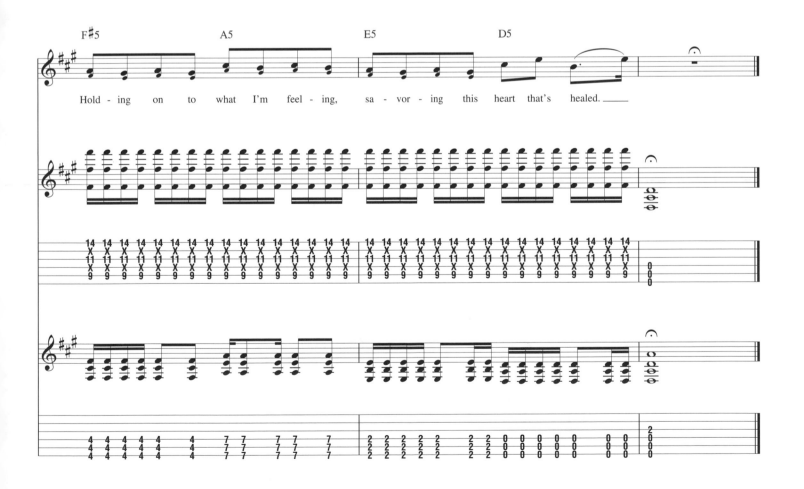

Hold - ing on to what I'm feel - ing, sa - vor - ing this heart that's healed. _____

Red Sam

**Words and Music by Sameer Bhattacharya, Jared Hartmann,
Kirkpatrick Seals, James Culpepper, Lacey Mosley and William Hoffman**

Drop D tuning:
(low to high) D-A-D-G-B-C

Intro
Moderately fast ♩ = 160

*Set for dotted-quarter note regeneration w/ 1 repeat.
Delay signal panned hard right w/ gradual fade out over next 6 meas.

**Chord symbols reflect overall harmony.

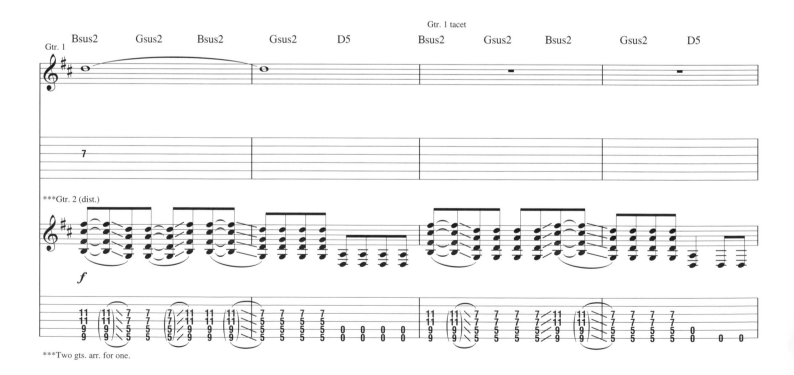

***Two gts. arr. for one.

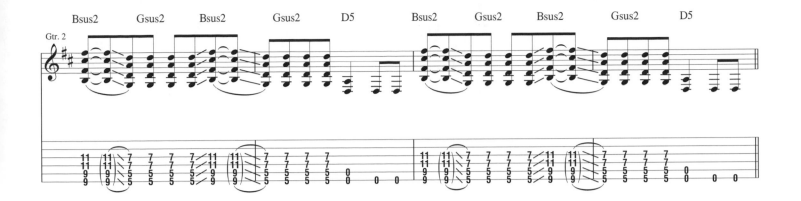

Verse

Half-time feel

1. Here ____ I ____ stand, ____ emp - ty ____ hands, ____ wish-ing my

wrists   were bleed - ing   to stop   the pain ___ from   the beat - ings.   Then   there _____   You _____   stood

hold - ing   me, _____   wait - ing   for   me   to   no - tice You.

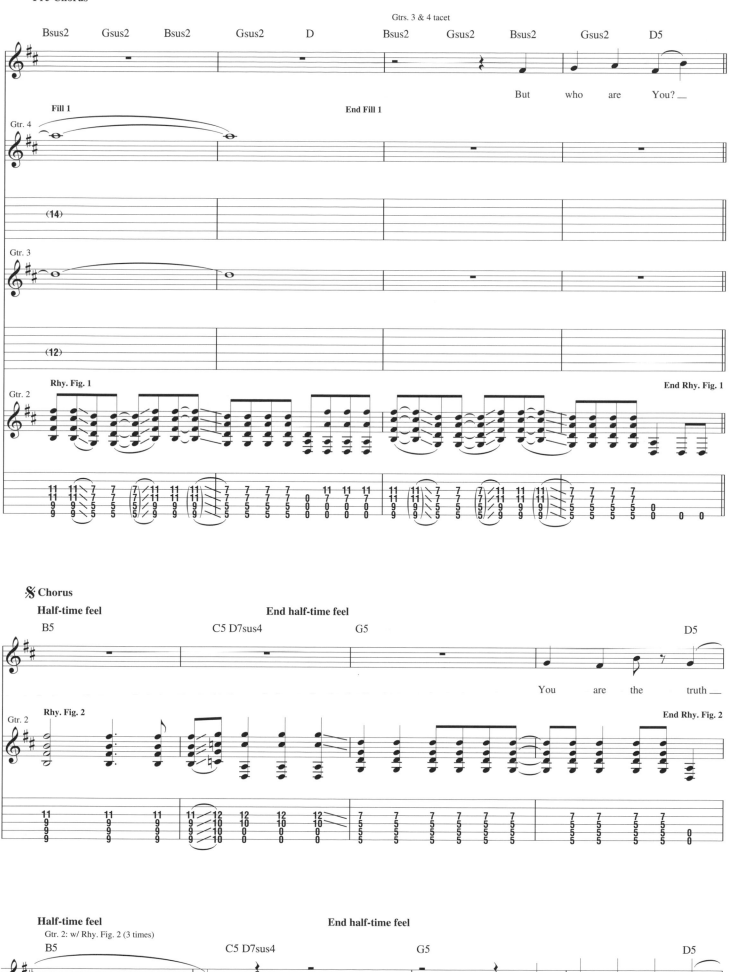

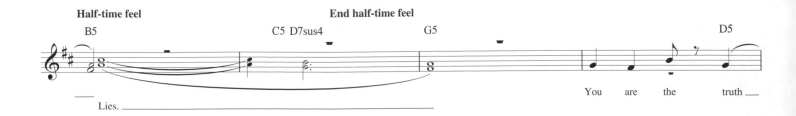

Half-time feel — End half-time feel

B5   C5   D7sus4   G5   D5

Lies.   You are the truth __

To Coda 1 ⊕
To Coda 2 ⊕

Half-time feel — End half-time feel

B5   C5   D7sus4   G5   D5

You are the truth.) __   sav - ing my life. __

Interlude

Gtr. 2: w/ Rhy. Fig. 1

Bsus2   Gsus2   Bsus2   Gsus2   D   Bsus2   Gsus2   Bsus2   Gsus2   D5

Verse

Half-time feel

Gtr. 4: w/ Riff A   Gtr. 2 tacet

Bm   G   Bm   G

2. The __ warmth __ of __   Your em - brace __

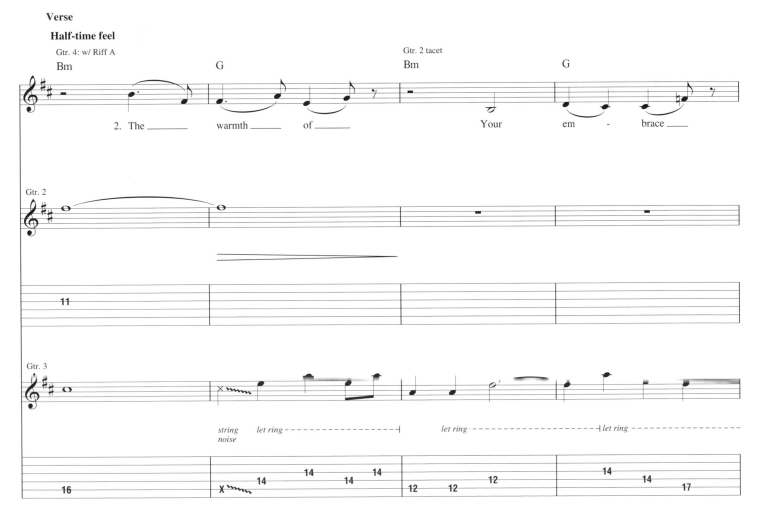

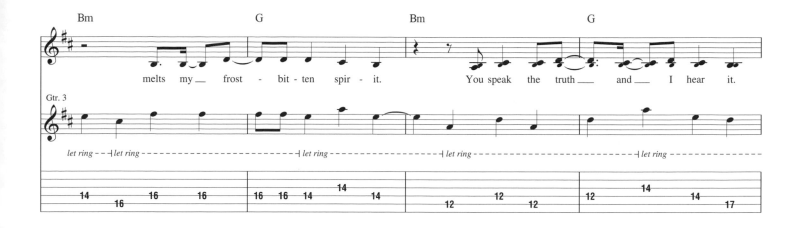

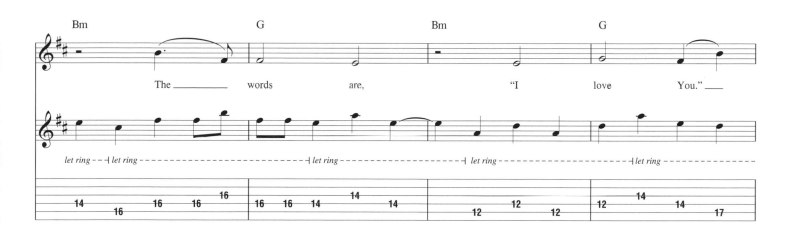

End half-time feel

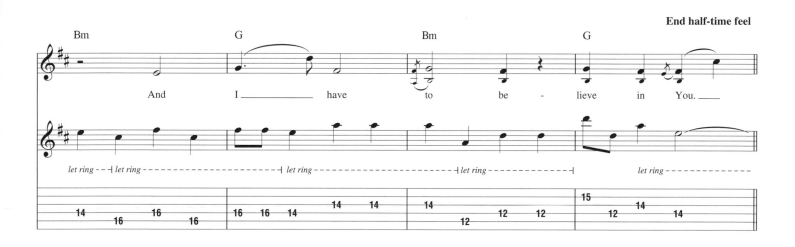

D.S. al Coda 1

Pre-Chorus

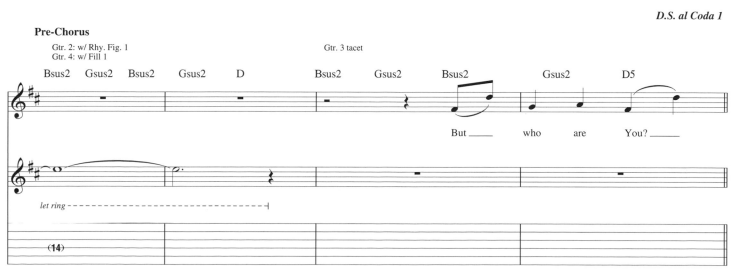

⊕ Coda 1

Bridge

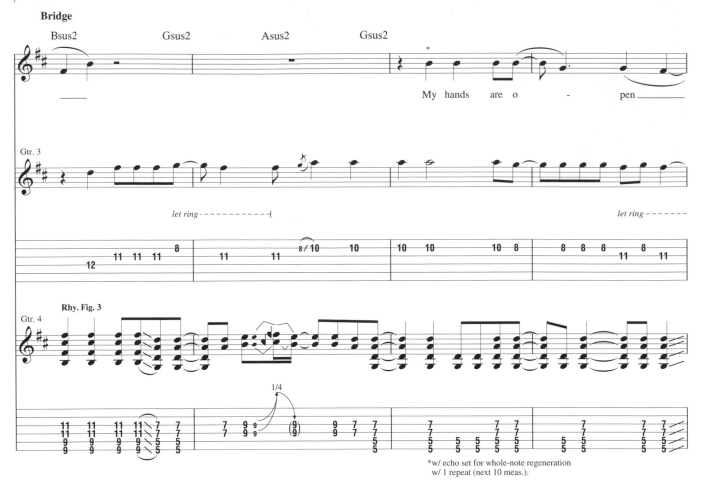

My hands are o - pen _____

*w/ echo set for whole-note regeneration
w/ 1 repeat (next 10 meas.).

and You are fill - ing them. _____

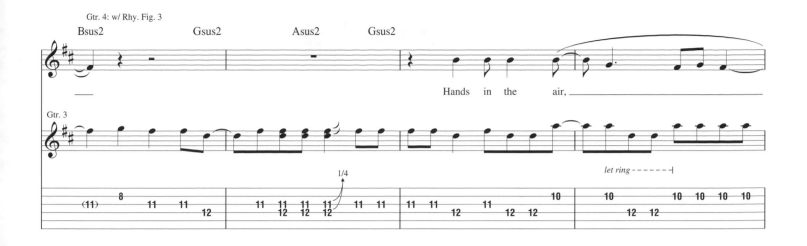

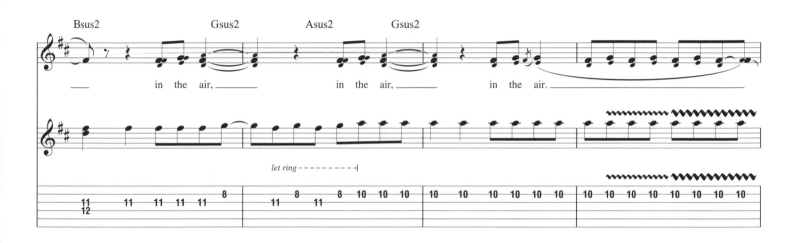

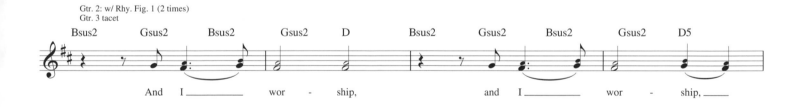

D.S. al Coda 2

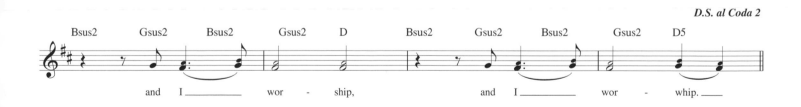

There for You

Words and Music by Sameer Bhattacharya, Jared Hartmann, Kirkpatrick Seals, James Culpepper and Lacey Mosley

Gtr. 3: Drop D tuning:
(low to high) D-A-D-G-B-E

*Chord symbols reflect basic harmony.

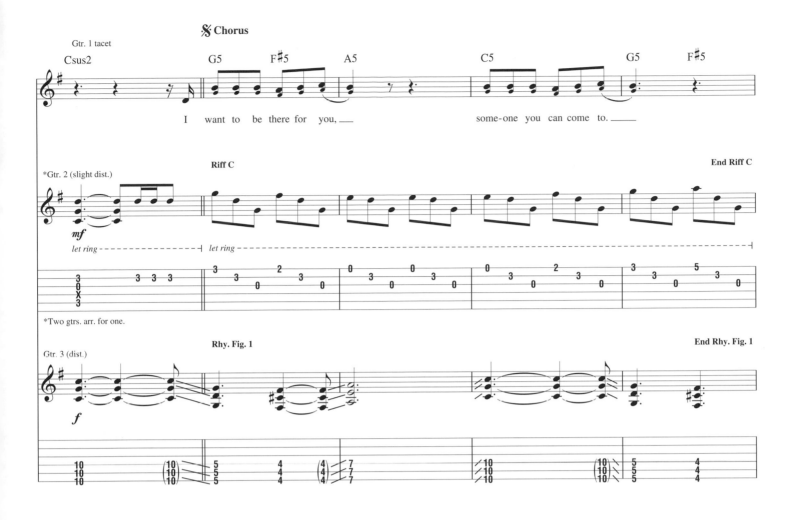

Verse

Gtr. 1: w/ Riff B (2 times)
Gtrs. 2 & 3 tacet

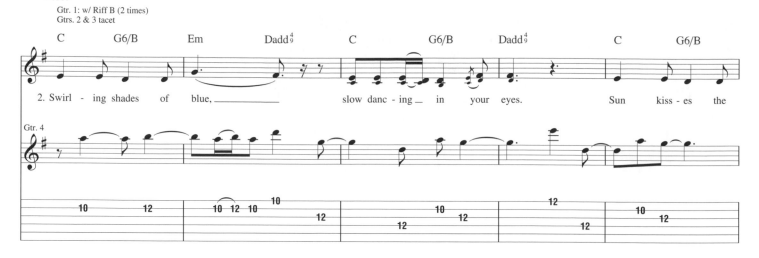

2. Swirl-ing shades of blue, ___ slow danc-ing ___ in your eyes. Sun kiss-es the

D.S. al Coda

earth ___ and I hush my ___ urge to cry, cry. ___ I

Coda

Bridge

'Cause I hear the whis-pered words in your mas-ter-piece beau-ti-ful. ___ You

*Composite arrangement

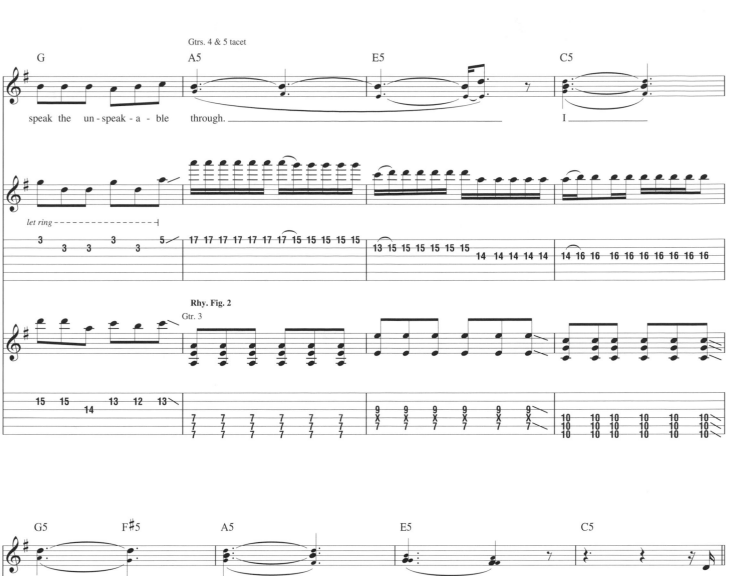

speak the un-speak-a-ble through. I

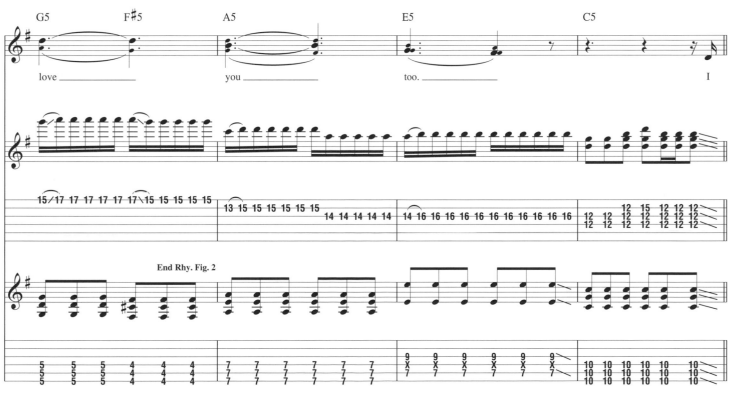

love you too. I

want to be there for you, some-one you can come to. I want to be there for you,

Chorus
Gtr. 2: w/ Riff C
Gtr. 3: w/ Rhy. Fig. 1

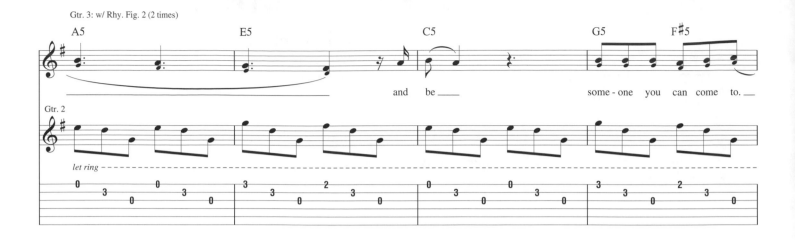

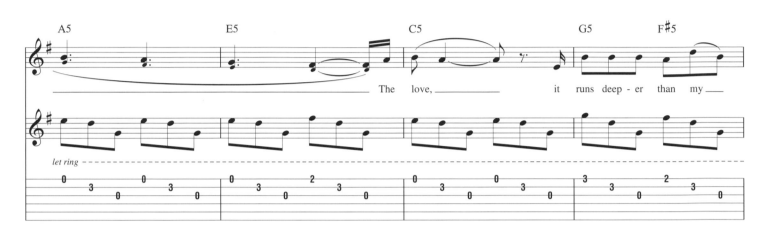

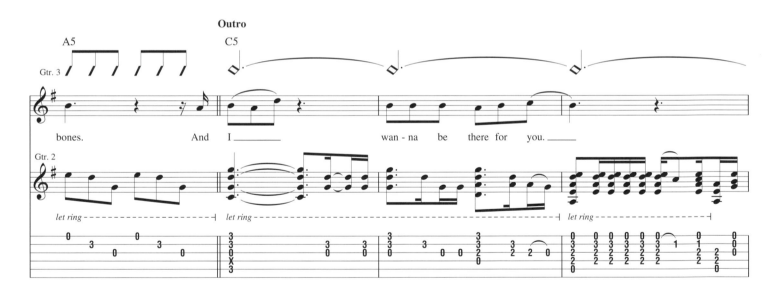

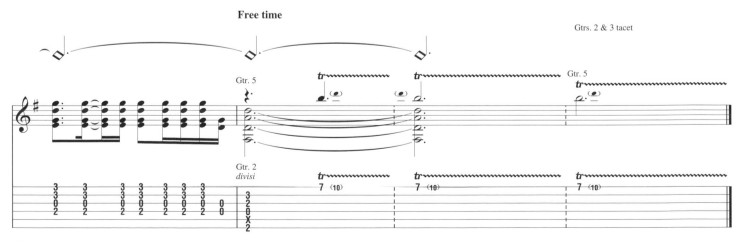

Breathe Today

**Words and Music by Sameer Bhattacharya, Jared Hartmann,
Kirkpatrick Seals, James Culpepper, Lacey Mosley and William Hoffman**

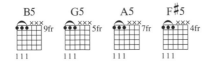

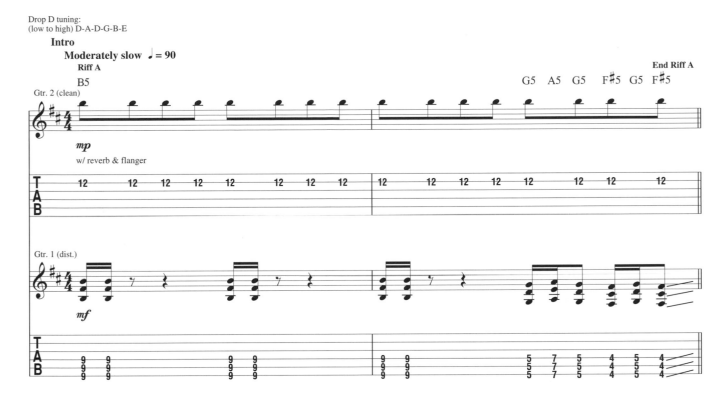

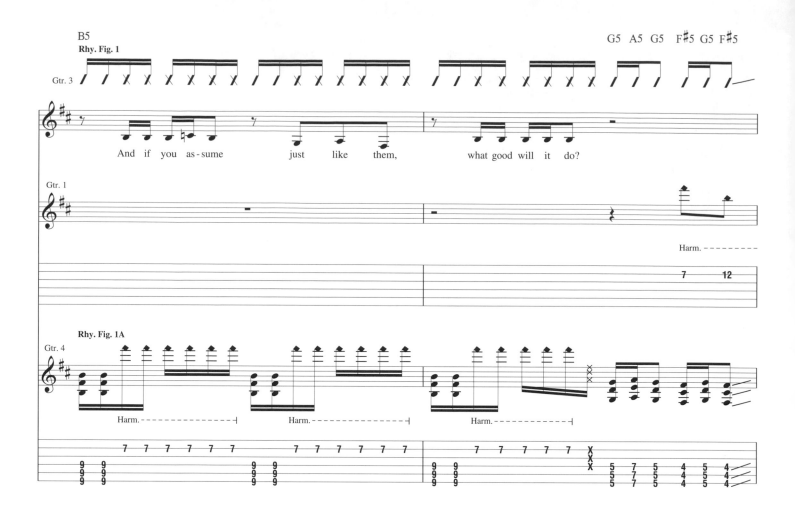

So find out for your-self   so your ig - no - rance   will stop bleed-ing through.

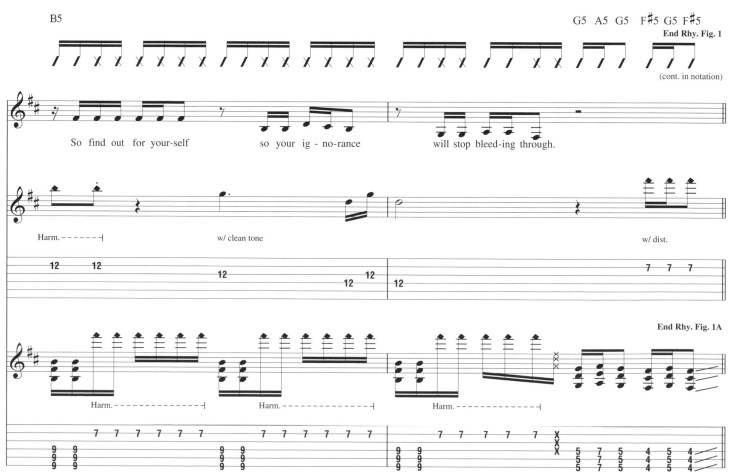

So find out for your-self   so your ig - no - rance   will stop bleed-ing through.

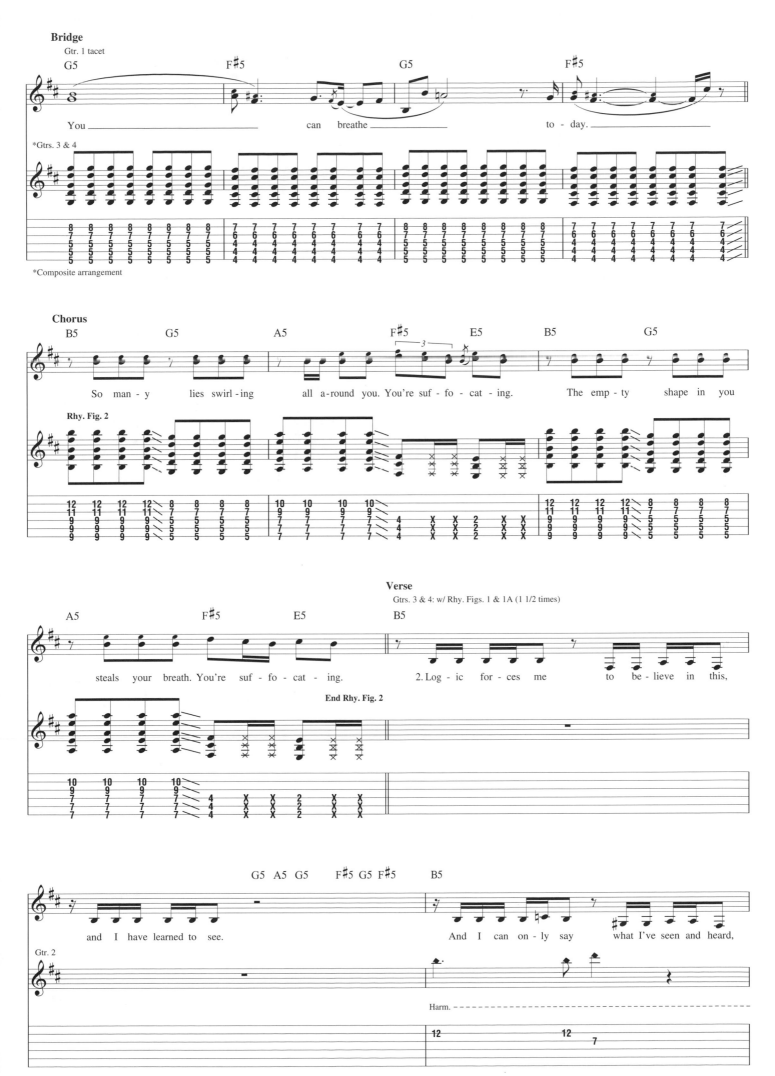

and on- ly you can choose.

And ev-'ry choice you make will af- fect you.

Bridge
Gtr. 2 tacet

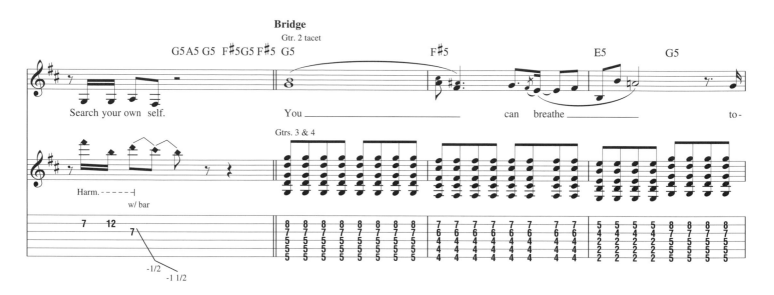

Search your own self.

You can breathe to-

Chorus

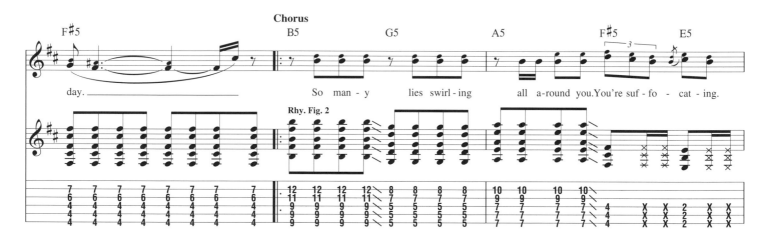

day.

So man- y lies swirl- ing all a-round you. You're suf- fo - cat - ing.

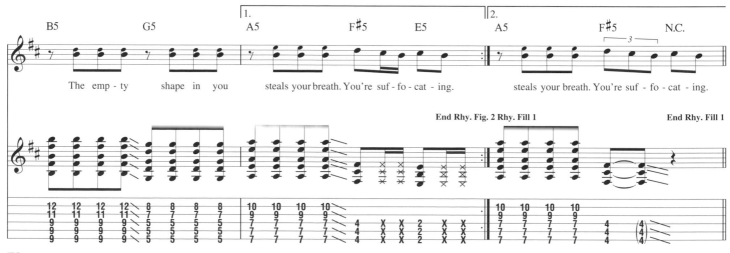

The emp- ty shape in you steals your breath. You're suf- fo- cat - ing.

steals your breath. You're suf- fo- cat - ing.

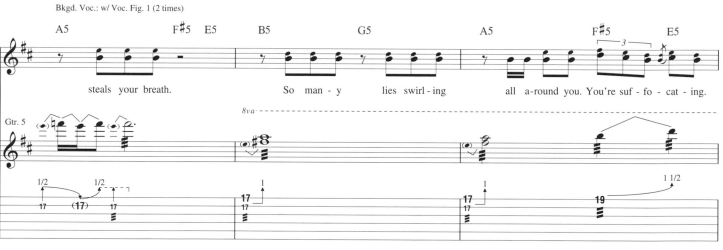

So I Thought

**Words and Music by Sameer Bhattacharya, Jared Hartmann,
Kirkpatrick Seals, James Culpepper, Lacey Mosley and William Hoffman**

Drop D tuning:
(low to high) D-A-D-G-B-E

Intro
Moderately slow ♩ = 86

*Chord symbols reflect basic harmony.

**Delay set for quarter-note regeneration w/ 1 repeat.
Delay signal panned hard left.

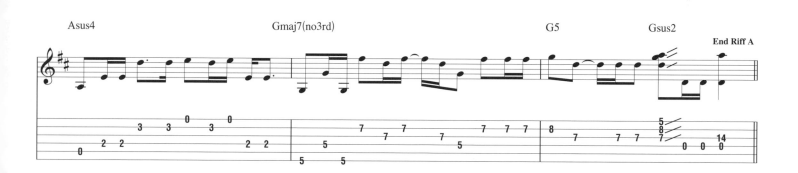

Verse
***Gtr. 1: w/ Riff A (1 1/3 times)

1. All your twist-ed thoughts _ free flow. To ev-er-last-ing mem-o-ries _ show soul. Kiss the

***delay off

†Delay set for eighth-note regeneration w/ 4 repeats.

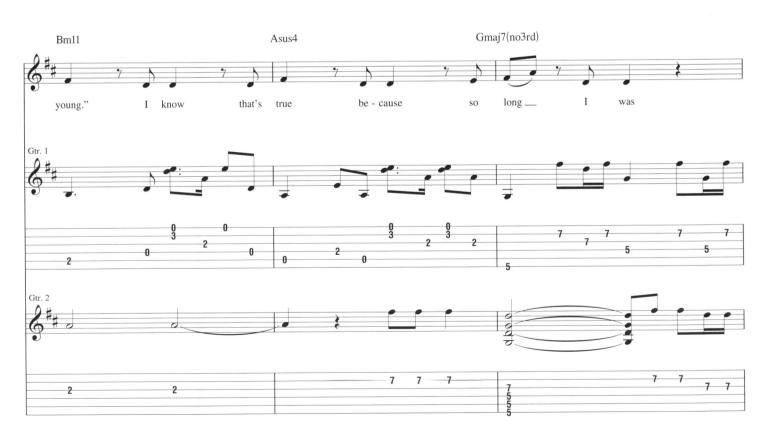

Bridge

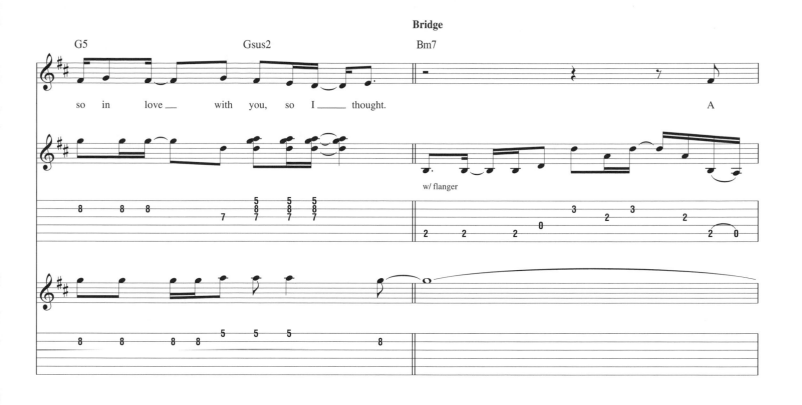

so in love ___ with you, so I ___ thought.

A

w/ flanger

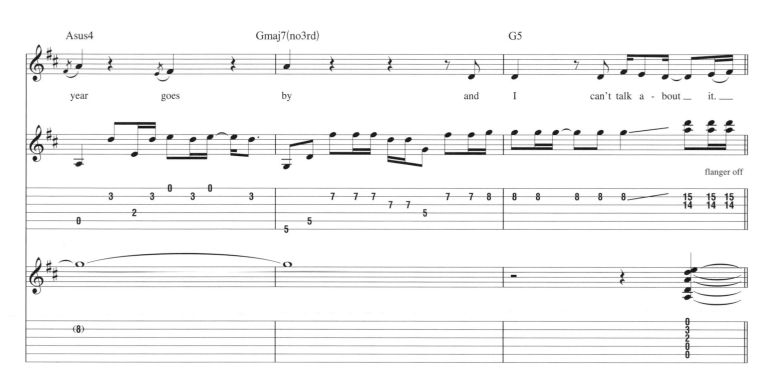

year goes by and I can't talk a-bout ___ it. ___

flanger off

Verse

Gtr. 1: w/ Riff A (1st 5 meas.)

2. On my knees, dim light-ed room, ___ thoughts free flow, try to con-sume ___ my-

Gtr. 2

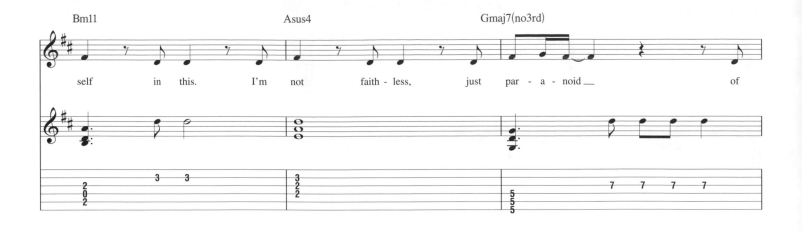

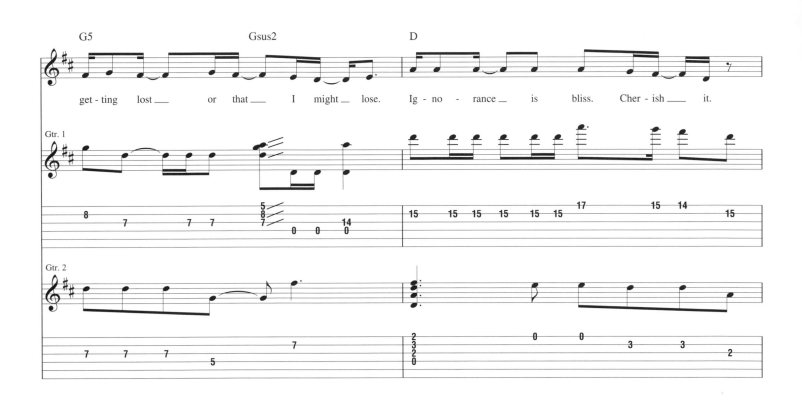

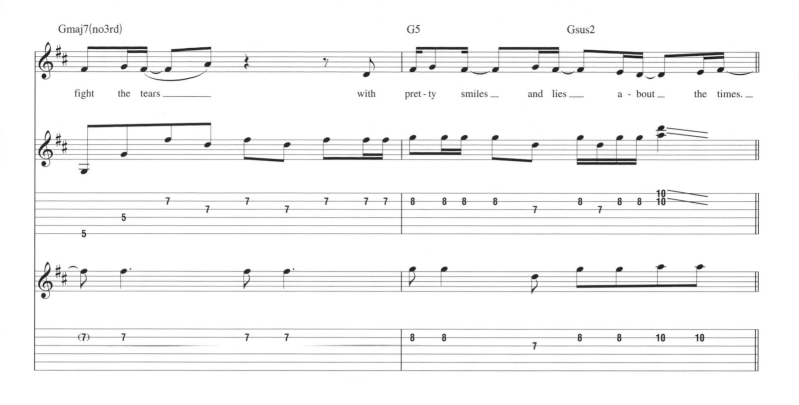

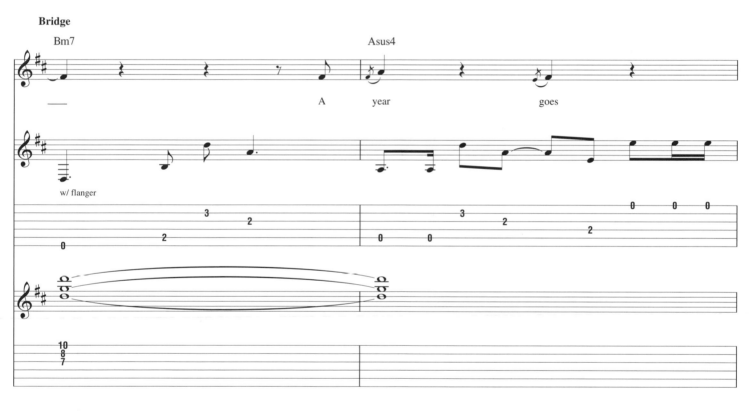

Bridge

Bm11   Asus4

The times weren't

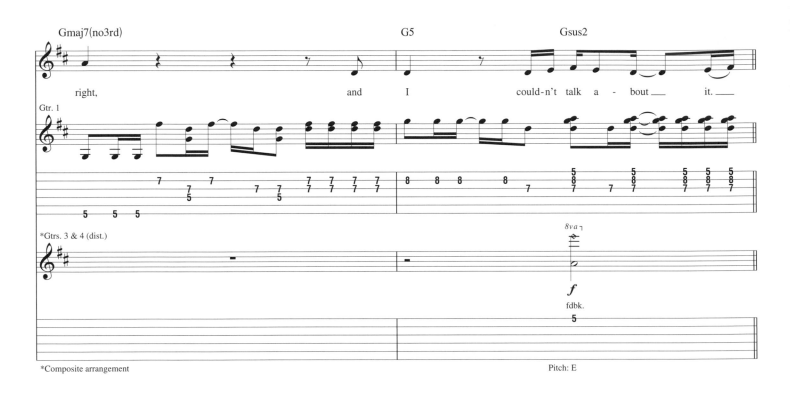

Gmaj7(no3rd)   G5   Gsus2

right, and I could-n't talk a - bout ___ it. ___

Gtr. 1

*Gtrs. 3 & 4 (dist.)

8va

f

fdbk.

*Composite arrangement   Pitch: E

𝄋 **Chorus**

Gtr. 1 tacet
2nd time, Gtr. 5: w/ Riff B

D   B5   G5

Cho - ris Ro - mance says, "Good - night." ___ Close your eyes ___ and I'll ___ close mine. Re -

Gtr. 5 (dist.)

mp

Rhy. Fig. 1
loco
Gtrs. 3 & 4

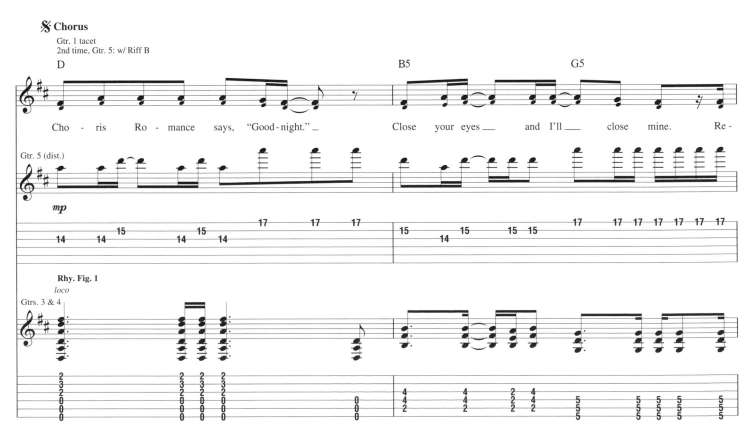

86

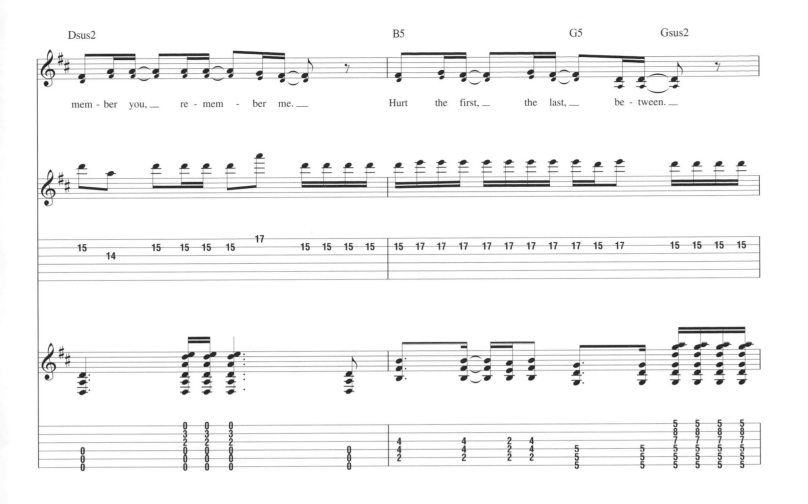

mem - ber you, __ re - mem - ber me. __ Hurt the first, __ the last, __ be - tween. __

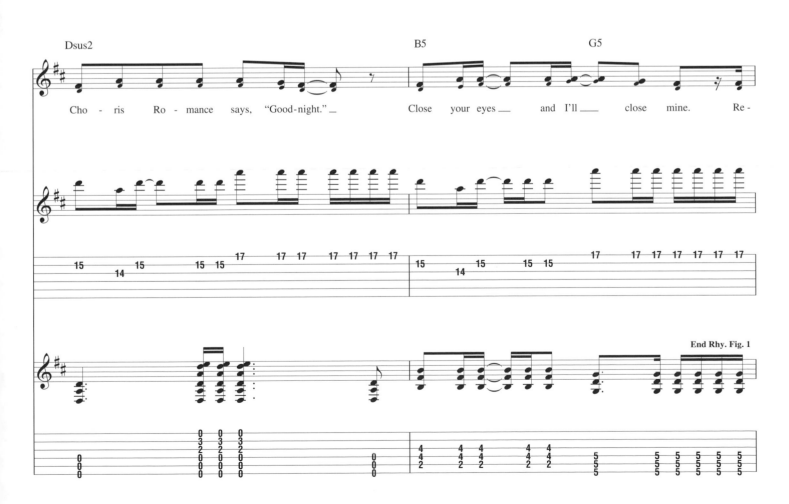

Cho - ris Ro - mance says, "Good-night." __ Close your eyes __ and I'll __ close mine. Re -

End Rhy. Fig. 1

To Coda ⊕

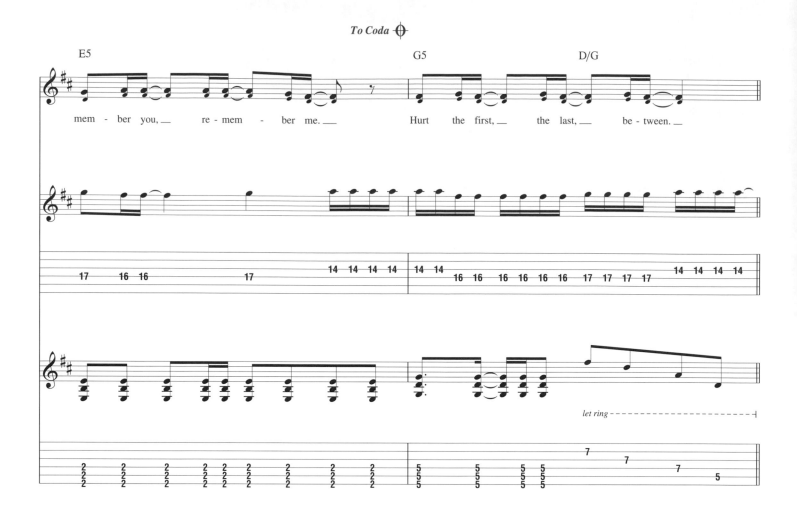

mem - ber you, __ re - mem - ber me. __ Hurt the first, __ the last, __ be - tween.

Bridge

Gtr. 5 tacet

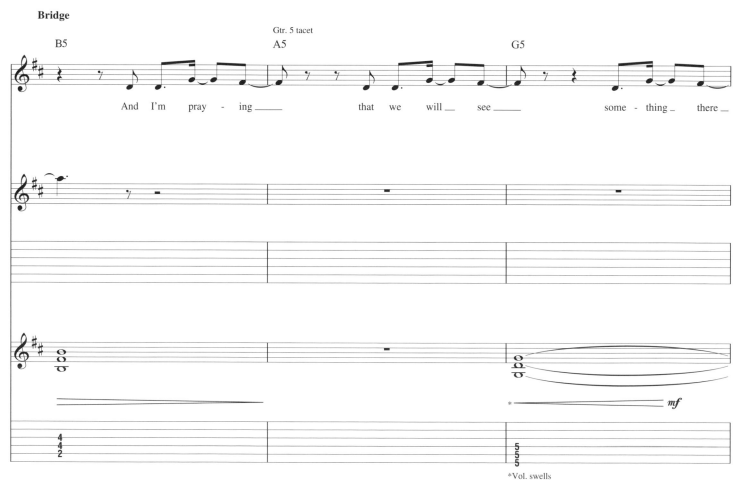

And I'm pray - ing _____ that we will __ see _____ some - thing _ there _

*Vol. swells

in be - tween ___ then and ___ there ___ that ex - ceeds ___

Gtr. 1

*Vol. swell

Gtr. 2

Gtrs. 3 & 4

G

___ all we can dream so we can talk a - bout ___ it.

Guitar Solo

Gtrs. 1 & 2 tacet
Gtrs. 3 & 4: w/ Rhy. Fig. 1

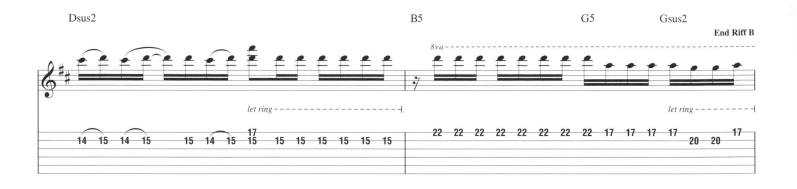

*Set for eighth-note regeneration w/ 2 repeats.

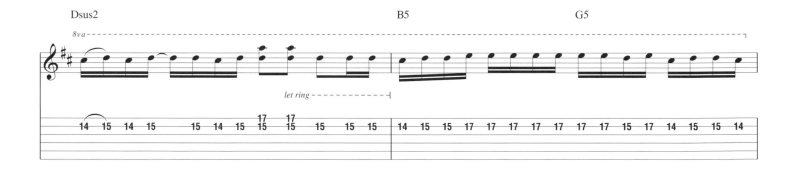

And all these twist-ed thoughts, __ I see

Je-sus there in be-tween. __ And all these twist-ed thoughts, __ I see

Free time

Fade out

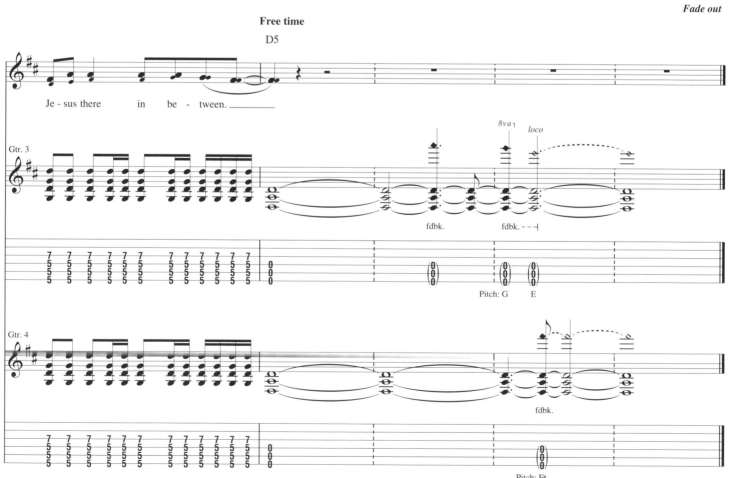

Je-sus there in be-tween. __

Guitar Notation Legend

Guitar music can be notated three different ways: on a *musical staff*, in *tablature*, and in *rhythm slashes*.

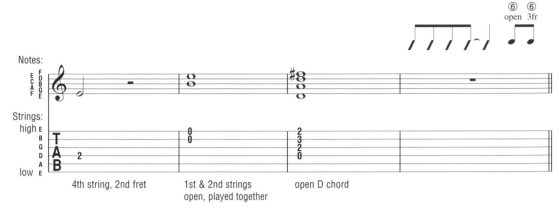

RHYTHM SLASHES are written above the staff. Strum chords in the rhythm indicated. Use the chord diagrams found at the top of the first page of the transcription for the appropriate chord voicings. Round noteheads indicate single notes.

THE MUSICAL STAFF shows pitches and rhythms and is divided by bar lines into measures. Pitches are named after the first seven letters of the alphabet.

TABLATURE graphically represents the guitar fingerboard. Each horizontal line represents a string, and each number represents a fret.

Definitions for Special Guitar Notation

HALF-STEP BEND: Strike the note and bend up 1/2 step.

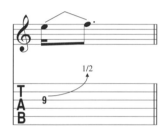

WHOLE-STEP BEND: Strike the note and bend up one step.

GRACE NOTE BEND: Strike the note and immediately bend up as indicated.

SLIGHT (MICROTONE) BEND: Strike the note and bend up 1/4 step.

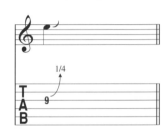

BEND AND RELEASE: Strike the note and bend up as indicated, then release back to the original note. Only the first note is struck.

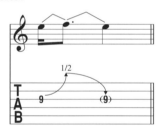

PRE-BEND: Bend the note as indicated, then strike it.

PRE-BEND AND RELEASE: Bend the note as indicated. Strike it and release the bend back to the original note.

UNISON BEND: Strike the two notes simultaneously and bend the lower note up to the pitch of the higher.

VIBRATO: The string is vibrated by rapidly bending and releasing the note with the fretting hand.

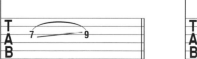

WIDE VIBRATO: The pitch is varied to a greater degree by vibrating with the fretting hand.

HAMMER-ON: Strike the first (lower) note with one finger, then sound the higher note (on the same string) with another finger by fretting it without picking.

PULL-OFF: Place both fingers on the notes to be sounded. Strike the first note and without picking, pull the finger off to sound the second (lower) note.

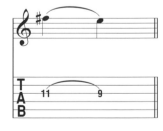

LEGATO SLIDE: Strike the first note and then slide the same fret-hand finger up or down to the second note. The second note is not struck.

SHIFT SLIDE: Same as legato slide, except the second note is struck.

TRILL: Very rapidly alternate between the notes indicated by continuously hammering on and pulling off.

TAPPING: Hammer ("tap") the fret indicated with the pick-hand index or middle finger and pull off to the note fretted by the fret hand.

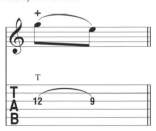

93

NATURAL HARMONIC: Strike the note while the fret-hand lightly touches the string directly over the fret indicated.

PINCH HARMONIC: The note is fretted normally and a harmonic is produced by adding the edge of the thumb or the tip of the index finger of the pick hand to the normal pick attack.

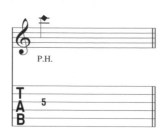

HARP HARMONIC: The note is fretted normally and a harmonic is produced by gently resting the pick hand's index finger directly above the indicated fret (in parentheses) while the pick hand's thumb or pick assists by plucking the appropriate string.

PICK SCRAPE: The edge of the pick is rubbed down (or up) the string, producing a scratchy sound.

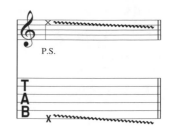

MUFFLED STRINGS: A percussive sound is produced by laying the fret hand across the string(s) without depressing, and striking them with the pick hand.

PALM MUTING: The note is partially muted by the pick hand lightly touching the string(s) just before the bridge.

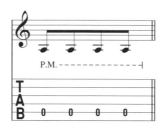

RAKE: Drag the pick across the strings indicated with a single motion.

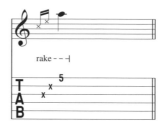

TREMOLO PICKING: The note is picked as rapidly and continuously as possible.

ARPEGGIATE: Play the notes of the chord indicated by quickly rolling them from bottom to top.

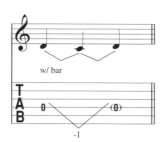

VIBRATO BAR DIVE AND RETURN: The pitch of the note or chord is dropped a specified number of steps (in rhythm), then returned to the original pitch.

VIBRATO BAR SCOOP: Depress the bar just before striking the note, then quickly release the bar.

VIBRATO BAR DIP: Strike the note and then immediately drop a specified number of steps, then release back to the original pitch.

Additional Musical Definitions

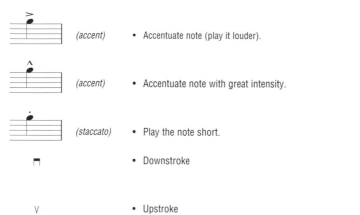

(accent)	•	Accentuate note (play it louder).
(accent)	•	Accentuate note with great intensity.
(staccato)	•	Play the note short.
⊓	•	Downstroke
V	•	Upstroke

D.S. al Coda
• Go back to the sign (𝄋), then play until the measure marked "**To Coda**," then skip to the section labelled "**Coda**."

D.C. al Fine
• Go back to the beginning of the song and play until the measure marked "**Fine**" (end).

Rhy. Fig.
• Label used to recall a recurring accompaniment pattern (usually chordal).

Riff
• Label used to recall composed, melodic lines (usually single notes) which recur.

Fill
• Label used to identify a brief melodic figure which is to be inserted into the arrangement.

Rhy. Fill
• A chordal version of a Fill.

tacet
• Instrument is silent (drops out).

• Repeat measures between signs.

• When a repeated section has different endings, play the first ending only the first time and the second ending only the second time.

NOTE: Tablature numbers in parentheses mean:
1. The note is being sustained over a system (note in standard notation is tied), or
2. The note is sustained, but a new articulation (such as a hammer-on, pull-off, slide or vibrato) begins, or
3. The note is a barely audible "ghost" note (note in standard notation is also in parentheses).

GUITAR *signature licks*

Signature Licks book/CD packs provide a step-by-step breakdown of "right from the record" riffs, licks, and solos so you can jam along with your favorite bands. They contain performance notes and an overview of each artist's or group's style, with note-for-note transcriptions in notes and tab. The CDs feature full-band demos at both normal and slow speeds.

BEST OF ACOUSTIC GUITAR
00695640 ....$19.95

AEROSMITH 1973-1979
00695106 ....$22.95

AEROSMITH 1979-1998
00695219 ....$22.95

BEST OF AGGRO-METAL
00695592 ....$19.95

BEST OF CHET ATKINS
00695752 ....$22.95

THE BEACH BOYS DEFINITIVE COLLECTION
00695683 ....$22.95

BEST OF THE BEATLES FOR ACOUSTIC GUITAR
00695453 ....$22.95

THE BEATLES BASS
00695283 ....$22.95

THE BEATLES FAVORITES
00695096 ....$24.95

THE BEATLES HITS
00695049 ....$24.95

BEST OF GEORGE BENSON
00695418 ....$22.95

BEST OF BLACK SABBATH
00695249 ....$22.95

BEST OF BLINK - 182
00695704 ....$22.95

BEST OF BLUES GUITAR
00695846 ....$19.95

BLUES GUITAR CLASSICS
00695177 ....$19.95

BLUES/ROCK GUITAR MASTERS
00695348 ....$19.95

BEST OF CHARLIE CHRISTIAN
00695584 ....$22.95

BEST OF ERIC CLAPTON
00695038 ....$24.95

ERIC CLAPTON – THE BLUESMAN
00695040 ....$22.95

ERIC CLAPTON – FROM THE ALBUM UNPLUGGED
00695250 ....$24.95

BEST OF CREAM
00695251 ....$22.95

DEEP PURPLE – GREATEST HITS
00695625 ....$22.95

THE BEST OF DEF LEPPARD
00696516 ....$22.95

THE DOORS
00695373 ....$22.95

FAMOUS ROCK GUITAR SOLOS
00695590 ....$19.95

BEST OF FOO FIGHTERS
00695481 ....$22.95

GREATEST GUITAR SOLOS OF ALL TIME
00695301 ....$19.95

BEST OF GRANT GREEN
00695747 ....$22.95

GUITAR INSTRUMENTAL HITS
00695309 ....$19.95

GUITAR RIFFS OF THE '60S
00695218 ....$19.95

BEST OF GUNS N' ROSES
00695183 ....$22.95

HARD ROCK SOLOS
00695591 ....$19.95

JIMI HENDRIX
00696560 ....$24.95

HOT COUNTRY GUITAR
00695580 ....$19.95

BEST OF JAZZ GUITAR
00695586 ....$24.95

ERIC JOHNSON
00699317 ....$22.95

ROBERT JOHNSON
00695264 ....$22.95

THE ESSENTIAL ALBERT KING
00695713 ....$22.95

B.B. KING – THE DEFINITIVE COLLECTION
00695635 ....$22.95

THE KINKS
00695553 ....$22.95

BEST OF KISS
00699413 ....$22.95

MARK KNOPFLER
00695178 ....$22.95

BEST OF YNGWIE MALMSTEEN
00695669 ....$22.95

BEST OF PAT MARTINO
00695632 ....$22.95

MEGADETH
00695041 ....$22.95

WES MONTGOMERY
00695387 ....$22.95

BEST OF NIRVANA
00695483 ....$24.95

THE OFFSPRING
00695852 ....$24.95

VERY BEST OF OZZY OSBOURNE
00695431 ....$22.95

BEST OF JOE PASS
00695730 ....$22.95

PINK FLOYD – EARLY CLASSICS
00695566 ....$22.95

THE POLICE
00695724 ....$22.95

THE GUITARS OF ELVIS
00696507 ....$22.95

BEST OF QUEEN
00695097 ....$22.95

BEST OF RAGE AGAINST THE MACHINE
00695480 ....$22.95

RED HOT CHILI PEPPERS
00695173 ....$22.95

RED HOT CHILI PEPPERS – GREATEST HITS
00695828 ....$24.95

BEST OF DJANGO REINHARDT
00695660 ....$22.95

BEST OF ROCK
00695884 ....$19.95

BEST OF ROCK 'N' ROLL GUITAR
00695559 ....$19.95

BEST OF ROCKABILLY GUITAR
00695785 ....$19.95

THE ROLLING STONES
00695079 ....$22.95

BEST OF JOE SATRIANI
00695216 ....$22.95

BEST OF SILVERCHAIR
00695488 ....$22.95

THE BEST OF SOUL GUITAR
00695703 ....$19.95

BEST OF SOUTHERN ROCK
00695703 ....$19.95

ROD STEWART
00695663 ....$22.95

BEST OF SYSTEM OF A DOWN
00695788 ....$22.95

STEVE VAI
00673247 ....$22.95

STEVE VAI – ALIEN LOVE SECRETS: THE NAKED VAMPS
00695223 ....$22.95

STEVE VAI – FIRE GARDEN: THE NAKED VAMPS
00695166 ....$22.95

STEVE VAI – THE ULTRA ZONE: NAKED VAMPS
00695684 ....$22.95

STEVIE RAY VAUGHAN
00699316 ....$24.95

THE GUITAR STYLE OF STEVIE RAY VAUGHAN
00695155 ....$24.95

BEST OF THE VENTURES
00695772 ....$19.95

THE WHO
00695561 ....$22.95

BEST OF ZZ TOP
00695738 ....$22.95

Complete descriptions and songlists online!

0606

RECORDED VERSIONS®
The Best Note-For-Note Transcriptions Available

ALL BOOKS INCLUDE TABLATURE

00692015	Aerosmith – Greatest Hits $22.95
00690603	Aerosmith – O Yeah! (Ultimate Hits) $24.95
00690178	Alice in Chains – Acoustic $19.95
00694865	Alice in Chains – Dirt $19.95
00690387	Alice in Chains – Nothing Safe: The Best of the Box $19.95
00690812	All American Rejects – Move Along $19.95
00694932	Allman Brothers Band – Volume 1 . . . . . .$24.95
00694933	Allman Brothers Band – Volume 2 . . . . . .$24.95
00694934	Allman Brothers Band – Volume 3 . . . . . .$24.95
00690755	Alter Bridge – One Day Remains $19.95
00690609	Audioslave $19.95
00690804	Audioslave – Out of Exile $19.95
00690366	Bad Company – Original Anthology, Book 1 . . .$19.95
00690503	Beach Boys – Very Best of $19.95
00690489	Beatles – 1 . . . .$24.95
00694929	Beatles – 1962-1966 . . . .$24.95
00694930	Beatles – 1967-1970 . . . .$24.95
00694832	Beatles – For Acoustic Guitar $22.95
00690110	Beatles – White Album (Book 1) $19.95
00690792	Beck – Guero $19.95
00692385	Berry, Chuck $19.95
00692200	Black Sabbath – We Sold Our Soul for Rock 'N' Roll $19.95
00690674	Blink-182 . . . .$19.95
00690389	Blink-182 – Enema of the State $19.95
00690523	Blink-182 – Take Off Your Pants & Jacket . .$19.95
00690491	Bowie, David – Best of $19.95
00690764	Breaking Benjamin – We Are Not Alone . .$19.95
00690451	Buckley, Jeff – Collection $24.95
00690590	Clapton, Eric – Anthology $29.95
00690415	Clapton Chronicles – Best of Eric Clapton . .$18.95
00690074	Clapton, Eric – The Cream of Clapton . . .$24.95
00690716	Clapton, Eric – Me and Mr. Johnson $19.95
00694869	Clapton, Eric – Unplugged $22.95
00690162	Clash – Best of The $19.95
00690593	Coldplay – A Rush of Blood to the Head . .$19.95
00690806	Coldplay – X & Y $19.95
00694940	Counting Crows – August & Everything After . .$19.95
00690401	Creed – Human Clay $19.95
00690352	Creed – My Own Prison $19.95
00690551	Creed – Weathered $19.95
00690648	Croce, Jim – Very Best of $19.95
00690572	Cropper, Steve – Soul Man $19.95
00690613	Crosby, Stills & Nash – Best of $19.95
00690777	Crossfade $19.95
00690289	Deep Purple – Best of $17.95
00690347	Doors, The – Anthology $22.95
00690348	Doors, The – Essential Guitar Collection . .$16.95
00690810	Fall Out Boy – From Under the Cork Tree . .$19.95
00690664	Fleetwood Mac – Best of $19.95
00690808	Foo Fighters – In Your Honor $19.95
00694920	Free – Best of $19.95
00690773	Good Charlotte – The Chronicles of Life and Death $19.95
00690601	Good Charlotte – The Young and the Hopeless $19.95
00690697	Hall, Jim – Best of $19.95
00694798	Harrison, George – Anthology $19.95
00690778	Hawk Nelson – Letters to the President . .$19.95
00692930	Hendrix, Jimi – Are You Experienced? . . .$24.95
00692931	Hendrix, Jimi – Axis: Bold As Love $22.95
00690608	Hendrix, Jimi – Blue Wild Angel $24.95
00692932	Hendrix, Jimi – Electric Ladyland $24.95
00690017	Hendrix, Jimi – Live at Woodstock $24.95

00690602	Hendrix, Jimi – Smash Hits $19.95
00690692	Idol, Billy – Very Best of $19.95
00690688	Incubus – A Crow Left of the Murder $19.95
00690457	Incubus – Make Yourself $19.95
00690544	Incubus – Morningview $19.95
00690730	Jackson, Alan – Guitar Collection $19.95
00690721	Jet – Get Born $19.95
00690684	Jethro Tull – Aqualung $19.95
00690647	Jewel – Best of $19.95
00690751	John5 – Vertigo $19.95
00690271	Johnson, Robert – New Transcriptions . . .$24.95
00699131	Joplin, Janis – Best of $19.95
00690427	Judas Priest – Best of $19.95
00690742	Killers, The – Hot Fuss $19.95
00690903	Kiss – Best of $24.95
00690780	Korn – Greatest Hits, Volume 1 . . . .$22.95
00690726	Lavigne, Avril – Under My Skin $19.95
00690679	Lennon, John – Guitar Collection $19.95
00690785	Limp Bizkit – Best of $19.95
00690781	Linkin Park – Hybrid Theory $22.95
00690782	Linkin Park – Meteora $22.95
00690783	Live, Best of $19.95
00690743	Los Lonely Boys $19.95
00690720	Lostprophets – Start Something $19.95
00694954	Lynyrd Skynyrd – New Best of $19.95
00690577	Malmsteen, Yngwie – Anthology $24.95
00690754	Manson, Marilyn – Lest We Forget $19.95
00694956	Marley, Bob – Legend $19.95
00694945	Marley, Bob – Songs of Freedom $24.95
00690748	Maroon5 – 1.22.03 Acoustic $19.95
00690657	Maroon5 – Songs About Jane $19.95
00120080	McLean, Don – Songbook $19.95
00694951	Megadeth – Rust in Peace $22.95
00690768	Megadeth – The System Has Failed $19.95
00690505	Mellencamp, John – Guitar Collection $19.95
00690646	Metheny, Pat – One Quiet Night $19.95
00690565	Metheny, Pat – Rejoicing $19.95
00690558	Metheny, Pat – Trio: 99>00 . . . .$19.95
00690561	Metheny, Pat – Trio > Live $22.95
00690040	Miller, Steve, Band – Young Hearts $19.95
00690769	Modest Mouse – Good News for People Who Love Bad News $19.95
00690786	Mudvayne – The End of All Things to Come . .$22.95
00690787	Mudvayne – L.D. 50 . . . .$22.95
00690794	Mudvayne – Lost and Found $19.95
00690611	Nirvana $22.95
00694883	Nirvana – Nevermind $19.95
00690026	Nirvana – Unplugged in New York $19.95
00690739	No Doubt – Rock Steady $22.95
00690807	Offspring, The – Greatest Hits $19.95
00694847	Osbourne, Ozzy – Best of $22.95
00690399	Osbourne, Ozzy – Ozzman Cometh $19.95
00694855	Pearl Jam – Ten $19.95
00690439	Perfect Circle, A – Mer De Noms $19.95
00690661	Perfect Circle, A – Thirteenth Step $19.95
00690499	Petty, Tom – Definitive Guitar Collection . .$19.95
00690731	Pillar – Where Do We Go from Here? $19.95
00690428	Pink Floyd – Dark Side of the Moon $19.95
00693864	Police, The – Best of $19.95
00694975	Queen – Greatest Hits $24.95
00690670	Queensryche – Very Best of $19.95
00694910	Rage Against the Machine $19.95
00690055	Red Hot Chili Peppers – Bloodsugarsexmagik $19.95
00690584	Red Hot Chili Peppers – By the Way $19.95

00690379	Red Hot Chili Peppers – Californication . .$19.95
00690673	Red Hot Chili Peppers – Greatest Hits $19.95
00690511	Reinhardt, Django – Definitive Collection . .$19.95
00690779	Relient K – MMHMM $19.95
00690643	Relient K – Two Lefts Don't Make a Right...But Three Do $19.95
00690631	Rolling Stones – Guitar Anthology $24.95
00690685	Roth, David Lee – Eat 'Em and Smile $19.95
00690694	Roth, David Lee – Guitar Anthology $24.95
00690749	Saliva – Survival of the Sickest $19.95
00690031	Santana's Greatest Hits $19.95
00690796	Schenker, Michael – Very Best of $19.95
00690566	Scorpions – Best of $19.95
00690604	Seger, Bob – Guitar Collection $19.95
00690530	Slipknot – Iowa $19.95
00690733	Slipknot – Vol. 3 (The Subliminal Verses) . .$19.95
00690691	Smashing Pumpkins Anthology $19.95
00120004	Steely Dan – Best of $24.95
00694921	Steppenwolf – Best of $22.95
00690655	Stern, Mike – Best of $19.95
00690689	Story of the Year – Page Avenue $19.95
00690520	Styx Guitar Collection $19.95
00120081	Sublime $19.95
00690519	SUM 41 – All Killer No Filler $19.95
00690771	SUM 41 – Chuck $19.95
00690767	Switchfoot – The Beautiful Letdown $19.95
00690815	Switchfoot – Nothing Is Sound $19.95
00690799	System of a Down – Mezmerize $19.95
00690531	System of a Down – Toxicity $19.95
00694824	Taylor, James – Best of $16.95
00690737	3 Doors Down – The Better Life $22.95
00690776	3 Doors Down – Seventeen Days $19.95
00690683	Trower, Robin – Bridge of Sighs $19.95
00690740	Twain, Shania – Guitar Collection $19.95
00699191	U2 – Best of: 1980-1990 . . . .$19.95
00690732	U2 – Best of: 1990-2000 . . . .$19.95
00690775	U2 – How to Dismantle an Atomic Bomb . .$22.95
00694411	U2 – The Joshua Tree $19.95
00660137	Vai, Steve – Passion & Warfare $24.95
00690370	Vaughan, Stevie Ray and Double Trouble – The Real Deal: Greatest Hits Volume 2 . .$22.95
00690116	Vaughan, Stevie Ray – Guitar Collection . . .$24.95
00660058	Vaughan, Stevie Ray – Lightnin' Blues 1983-1987 . . . .$24.95
00694835	Vaughan, Stevie Ray – The Sky Is Crying . .$22.95
00690015	Vaughan, Stevie Ray – Texas Flood $19.95
00690772	Velvet Revolver – Contraband $22.95
00690071	Weezer (The Blue Album) $19.95
00690800	Weezer – Make Believe $19.95
00690447	Who, The – Best of $24.95
00690672	Williams, Dar – Best of $19.95
00690710	Yellowcard – Ocean Avenue $19.95
00690589	ZZ Top Guitar Anthology $22.95